Johnny Giles and John McGovern in action

THE ALL STARS FOOTBALL BOOK No. 13

edited by
COLIN TODD

with special contributions by

IAN CALLAGHAN
MIKE CHANNON
ALLAN CLARKE
STEVE HEIGHWAY
GORDON JEFFERY
JULIAN JEFFERY
BOB LATCHFORD
STAN LIVERSEDGE
RODNEY MARSH
STEVE PERRYMAN
JOE ROYLE
HARRY STANLEY
NOBBY STILES
COLIN TODD

WORLD DISTRIBUTORS, PUBLISHERS, LONDON

*First Published by World Distributors, Publishers,
London*

*I.B.M. Computer Typesetting by Print Origination, Liverpool, England
Printed and bound in Holland*

To Dean from Grandad 1974

CONTENTS

Picture Selections by GORDON JEFFERY

LIST OF ILLUSTRATIONS

A Progress Report from COLIN TODD

Mud-splattered Colin Todd and Charlie George in action

I WISH THE CRITICS WOULD TRY TO UNDERSTAND HOW PHYSICALLY AND MENTALLY EXHAUSTED PLAYERS ARE AFTER A LONG SEASON

A lot has happened since a year ago I prepared my first article as the new editor of ALL STARS. I think most of you know that the articles in this, and all annuals and bound books, have to be with the printers quite a long time before the book is actually published.

The time between writing and selling is not so

long with magazines of course. They are not bound with stiff covers; they have less pages; and are not presented in the same way as annuals. Even so I expect you have bought a magazine that has just come out and read an article by a player about *his* club when, in fact, he had been transferred to a different club perhaps a week before! Or, more sadly, read something about a match he was very much looking forward to playing in but you know when you get the magazine, what he did not when he wrote his article, that he had been injured rather badly.

You will understand then that when I was writing for you a year ago, my club Derby County were moving along comfortably in the First Division but few people, outside of the club and our supporters, were tipping us to win the Football League Championship.

You may remember that Sheffield United had started off the season with quite a bang but by the midway stage they had dropped back—to a large extent probably because Trevor Hockey had been injured, and however good the reserve cover in a club, key players, as he was for Sheffield United, cannot be completely replaced. After all if a reserve player was as good as the best player, or one of the best players, in a first team, he would not still be a reserve player! (The one possible exception would be in the case of a goalkeeper but even then it is rare for two very good keepers to stay with the same club—usually one of them is transferred as, for example, Leicester a few years back were prepared to let Gordon Banks go to Stoke because they knew that Peter Shilton was ready to take over. Since then we have seen the position at Leeds where David Harvey for Scotland and Gary Sprake for Wales were both playing for the national teams in World Cup qualifying matches on the same evening last November—David Harvey against Denmark, and Gary Sprake against England.)

But, like we nearly all do when we are talking football, I have wandered away from my point about Sheffield United's faltering after a good start to the 1971-72 season. By the halfway stage the position at the top of the First Division was that Manchester United were the clear leaders with 33 points; their neighbours the City

had 29; Leeds, who over the past six or seven seasons have always been around the top, were third with 28 points; and we were tucked in with Liverpool in fourth place with 27 points. Then came Spurs and Sheffield United with 26 points and, in eighth place, Arsenal who the season before had done the 'impossible' League and Cup 'double'.

As I am sure you will remember Manchester United fell away very badly in the second half of the season. You may not realise just how badly—they gained 33 points in their first 21 matches but only 15 in the last 21 matches which was a pretty good indication that, unless the first team was considerably strengthened, United were going to be in trouble in 1972-73!

Arsenal improved in the second-half of the season—they got 28 points compared with 24 in the first-half, but they had been too far behind at the halfway mark to strongly challenge for the Championship unless the other leading clubs had all fallen away. In fact the other leaders— that is Manchester City, Leeds, Liverpool and, the one that most people forgot Derby—did not falter, and we had one of the most exciting finishes to the Football League First Division that there has ever been with the four clubs all 'in with a chance' with just nine important matches to be played that involved them.

The actual position was this:

	P	W	D	L	F	A	Pts
Derby County	40	23	10	7	68	31	56
Manchester City	40	22	11	7	74	43	55
Liverpool	39	23	8	8	62	29	54
Leeds United	38	22	9	7	69	28	53

We were at the top but Liverpool and Leeds had 'matches in hand'. It is an old football truth however that having the points is better than having the matches in hand. Our concern was whether we had enough points—and also how many more we could get from our last two matches both of which were against other possible champions!

Before we played again however Leeds and Manchester City had matches to play against Newcastle and Ipswich and our chances improved *without our playing* when Leeds (0-1) and City (1-2) were both beaten. Manchester

Colin Todd rises above Spurs' Martin Chivers

City then bounced back however by beating us 2-0 whilst Leeds beat West Bromwich Albion 1-0 and Liverpool beat Ipswich 2-0. That seemed a black Saturday for us with City on 57 points and all their 42 matches played; Liverpool (from 40 matches) and ourselves (from 41 matches) both on 56 points; and Leeds with 55 points from 40 matches. And next we had to finish our programme with a match against Liverpool—a match that gave us the chance to not only gain two valuable points for ourselves but also, of course, to reduce Liverpool's 'match-in-hand'

advantage. And we did win the match—by a single goal scored by John McGovern.

That win brought our season's tally of points up to 58 and meant that Manchester City (57 points) were out of the race. Liverpool were two points behind with one match to play—against Arsenal at Highbury. But the same evening that we beat Liverpool, Leeds had a 2-0 win over Chelsea so that Don Revie's boys had 57 points (one less than ourselves) with one match to play—against Wolves at Molyneux.

The problem for both Leeds and Liverpool

That mud again—John McGovern and Alan Ball in action

Derby in the European Cup with John O'Hare and two Zeljeznicar players in action in the home leg

was fixing the dates for their vital final matches. Liverpool were fortunate in that they were free from other committments but Leeds and Liverpool's last-match opponents Arsenal were the F.A. Cup finalists—due to be played on 6 May. And there was an England national team problem tied up with all this. A week before, England had lost 1-3 to West Germany at Wembley in the European Football Championship quarter-final when, after in any case five months absence from international football, they had had to field a side weakened by injuries that were the result of the hectic end-of-season league and cup matches. Now, a week after the Cup Final, England had to go to Berlin for the return match.

It was the Football League who stepped in and fixed the date for the last vital League championship matches. The matches had to be played on Monday 8 May—just two days after the Cup Final. I think everyone must have sympathised with Leeds' position and felt their annoyance justified. In a season stretching over more than nine months it does seem wrong that this sort of situation, when a club is asked to play two such important matches with only a Sunday between them, arises.

Still there it was—and meanwhile Derby were away in Majorca enjoying a 'working holiday,' and between our friendly matches we waited on the news from England and thought about all the possibilities.

Leeds won the Cup but lost big Mick Jones with a bad injury sustained in the last minute of the match. He was definitely a non-starter for the clash at Molyneux. Leeds' goal average compared with ours was such that if, by drawing with Wolves they gained just one point they would finish above us on goal average—unless that draw was by the absurd score of 11-11 or more!

Liverpool on the other hand needed to win to reach our total of 58 points but if they did this they too would finish above us on goal-average, but not, unless they won by some massive score, above Leeds—if Leeds got a point!

On the other hand it seemed possible that Liverpool might have an advantage in that their opponents, Arsenal, were the beaten Cup finalists. What affect would that defeat have on the London club? Would their disappointment show in their play? For that matter how much would Leeds be swept along by the thrill of having won the Cup? Would both Arsenal and Wolves, who had virtually nothing to gain themselves from the matches, show their pride by turning in the sort of performance you expect from sides challenging for honours?

Well I expect you know what did happen. The match at Highbury was goalless and at Wolverhampton goals from Munro and Dougan for the home side were countered by only one—by Billy Bremner—for Leeds. So, with one point more than our three rivals, Leeds, Liverpool and Manchester City, Derby County were the champions and we returned from Majorca in triumph.

But for several Derby players, including myself, the season was far from being over. Ray McFarland was the first in action—for England in that second leg match against West Germany. So too, of players involved in the vital Monday evening matches, were Paul Madeley and Norman Hunter of Leeds, Emlyn Hughes of Liverpool, and Peter Storey and Alan Ball of Arsenal. All of them had, of course, missed the beginning of England's week of training before the match (actually less than a week since time had to be taken out for travelling), and all —except Roy McFarland—must have felt some disappointment at having been beaten for the Championship or the Cup.

England drew that match—a good result in itself but, of course, not for the second leg after losing the first one. And there were more international matches to come—in the British Home Championship in which, of the Derby players,

Terry Hennessey and Alan Durban were in the Welsh squad, Archie Gemmill and John O'Hare with the Scots, and Roy McFarland and myself with the England party.

If the British Home Championship matches were less exciting, less entertaining than most people expect with only eight goals scored in six matches, I wish the critics would try to understand how physically and mentally exhausted players are after a long season. One of the most regular of England players in recent seasons was missing from the squad for example—not from an actual injury but from the sheer exhaustion that sent Francis Lee into the Bolton Royal Infirmary for observation after Manchester City's last match.

The British Home Championship matches were important to me because I played my first match for England in a Full international match. It was not, I am afraid, the happiest of matches to make a first appearance in, and an unfamiliar looking England team were beaten at Wembley by Northern Ireland. The Irish skipper Terry Neill got the only goal of the match so I suppose I could take some consolation from the fact that our defence, in which I played, was only penetrated once.

By this time I was not only ready for a break, I desperately needed it. I think you may remember that the F.A. had decided to call off any tour by the national squad after sounding the reactions of the players on the trip back from the second-leg match against West Germany in Berlin. But an Under-23 tour was still on and I was picked for this. We informed the F.A. that I was not fit for such a tour but, looking back, I suppose it would have been wiser to have got some definite medical evidence. This was however the close season and all I wanted was to rest and relax. I shall know better another time . . .

Another time? Of course I am looking forward to another time but meanwhile I can share in the enjoyment of Derby's play. A lot of people hinted—some of them did more than hint!—that we were less than deserving champions, and I think there were a few smirking faces when we showed in-and-out form at the start of the 1972-73 season. As to the European Champions Cup—that, it was suggested, would show our limitations!

Well, as I write we are in the last eight of that competition with an unforgettable performance against Benfica behind us—and don't think that this Benfica is inferior to past elevens of that club. If they are, there must be something amiss in Portugal since the Benfica club have got maximum points in the first-half of the league season in that country! And as we have progressed in the European competition, so has our league form gained in consistency with some peak performances, like the 5-0 trouncing of Arsenal, to let everyone know that we are a really top-class and entertaining club. By the time you read this you will know what the latter part of the season has brought Derby—and myself. I am confident it won't be bad!

Kevin Hector rounds Wolves' Gerry Taylor in a League match at the Baseball ground

Sir Alf Ramsey (but not the small boys!) watches Alan Ball at an England training session at Roehampton

Francis Lee in the England tracksuit

THREE Little WORDS
that led to a record by
Ian Callaghan

Ian Callaghan (right) challenges Arsenal's Alan Ball in last season's League match at Highbury

IF YOU'RE WONDERING HOW I'VE KEPT GOING SO LONG, I'LL GIVE YOU THE ANSWER IN THREE LITTLE WORDS. DEDICATION—AND LUCK

In the first week of September, 1972, I played in a second-round Football League Cup-tie at Carlisle—and went into the record books. For that game was my 533rd for Liverpool, and at the end of it, I had overtaken the club record of 532 matches which had been set—and held for years—by the great Billy Liddell, who was affectionately known as the Flying Scot and Mr. Liddellpool, when he was at the height of his fame at Anfield.

It was appropriate that Billy Liddell should finally surrender his record to me, in a way—and I DON'T want to sound big-headed about this. But the fact is that when I was an eager youngster first trying to make my way in football, Billy was my hero, just as Alan A'Court became my idol later on at Anfield. I never had any ideas about playing on the left wing, though—I kicked off as a right-half; and I certainly never had any notions of setting up club records for appearances. Take it from me, footballers don't think about records—especially when they're starting off in the game. I was satisfied to have but one ambition in those days soon after I had left school . . . and that was for Liverpool to decide that I was good enough to be allowed to stay at Anfield.

By the time I did overtake Billy Liddell's record, I had clocked up more than 50 F.A. Cup ties and almost half a century of European matches, played in two Championship-winning teams and two F.A. Cup Final teams, and in a European Cup-winners Cup Final. But all these things were in the undreamed-of future, when I left the recreation ground pitches of The Dingle to sample the real professional atmosphere of football that was Anfield. I was simply a Liverpool lad who had achieved his goal—to be signed on by Liverpool, the club of which he had been a fan.

Manager Bill Shankly—"the boss," as we call him—has been kind enough to say one or two nice things about me, in my time at Anfield. He recalls the days when I was an amateur, and he remembers, too, the fact that I was still a slimly-built lad even when I became a professional. "The boss" reckons that they didn't need to urge me to get stuck in, or do extra training . . . instead, they had to advise me to simmer down, as he puts it. I can tell you that whatever enthusiasm I showed in those days was spurred largely because I desperately wanted to show that I COULD make the grade.

It seems, when I look back, that Billy Liddell has played quite a part in my footballing life, for when I did break through to the first team, only six weeks after having signed as a professional, I took Billy's place in a game against Bristol Rovers at Anfield. It gave me a real kick to think I was playing in front of the famous Kop—and it also made me slightly apprehensive as to how I would fare. But it seems I did all right, by and large—I'm still there!

One of the early games, after Liverpool had won promotion from the Second Division, still sticks in my mind. And I know "the boss" hasn't forgotten it, either. For Liverpool were playing Manchester United at Old Trafford. And that was always an event. It still is, for that matter.

That day, I was given the job of marking a player whose name has long been a household word in football—Bobby Charlton. I was told to play deep, and make a point of keeping the ball away from Bobby, for we knew that if he were allowed to push the passes around—not to mention having a crack at goal with those famous feet—we could be letting ourselves in for all kinds of trouble. Well, I must have made a reasonable job of it, cutting out the supply of passes to Bobby, for we finished up by winning that game.

Of course, you always tend to remember games you have won, and the great seasons of your footballing life. Liverpool did a tremendous hat-trick during the 1960's, when they won the First Division title, the F.A. Cup, and the Championship again, from 1964 to 1966. I was proud to be a member of that great team . . . and there are still a few of them left at Anfield, such as Chris Lawler and Tommy Smith.

After more than half a century of games for Liverpool, I still think that my outstanding memory is of the F.A. Cup Final; for two reasons. When Liverpool defeated Leeds in 1965 at Wembley—and the game went to extra time, just as our final against Arsenal did, in 1971—it was the first time that the F.A. Cup had graced the boardroom sideboard at Anfield. And the second reason?—I like to think that I played a part in bringing the Cup to Anfield, because I slung over the cross which Ian St. John headed into the Leeds net, to make it 2-1 for Liverpool.

I took on and got past Leeds full-back Willie Bell, went to the bye-line, and pulled the ball back as a lowish cross for Ian to meet the ball and pop it into the net. What a moment that was! And I remember another of our heroes that day was left-back Gerry Byrne, who played through most of the match with a broken collar bone . . . and kept his injury a secret from our opponents until it was all over.

We came back from Wembley to Liverpool, and had a tremendous reception. Which brings

Tommy Smith, Albert Johanneson (Leeds) and Ian Callaghan in action in Liverpool's 1965 F.A. Cup Final victory

me to another great memory . . . our European Champions Cup semi-final against Inter-Milan, only a few days after our F.A. Cup triumph. People thought we might be shattered, after our efforts at Wembley; and I suppose we were, at that. But, somehow, we geared ourselves for this new challenge, and we went out and whipped Inter by three goals to one, while the Kop chanted "Go back to Italy!" to the tune of a Neapolitan folk song!

We really felt that it was going to be our year for the European Champions Cup, as well. But that was not to be. Things went against us, when we travelled to Italy for the return game. In the first place, we came up against the Italian fans— they besieged our hotel from morning till night . . . and even later. That made it difficult for us to get to sleep. And then there was the church-clock bell which kept on chiming every 15 minutes.

Finally, "the boss" went and got hold of the local priest, and tried to get the bell stopped, or at least muffled. But the priest solemnly informed him that this was impossible . . . the

Tommy Smith, Ian Callaghan and Chris Lawler—the three 'survivors' of the 1965 Cup winning team—taking part in a Sunday afternoon sponsored 'Pram Push' in aid of Leukaemia Research funds

clock had been chiming like that for a century or so, and we'd have to put up with it. Which we did.

As for the match itself, what a fiasco it turned out to be, for us. We lost, 3-0; but we wouldn't have felt so badly, had the goals been good ones. But if you ask anyone who played in that Liverpool team—yes, even today—they'll tell you: "We wuz robbed!" Two of Inter's goals came from refereeing decisions which amazed and appalled us. One was a direct free-kick which should never have been—and it brought

Inter a goal. And the other goal was one which I've never seen before or since.

The ball bounced into our half of the field, and ended up safely enough in the hands of our goalkeeper, Tommy Lawrence. He prepared to take the kick—he'd advanced a few yards off his line to collect the ball—and as he drew back his foot and got ready to release the ball from his hands, what happened?—An Inter player ran round the BACK of Tommy, and smartly kicked the ball from his hands, then stuck it into the net. And the referee said it was a goal. So we

Ray Clemence, Liverpool's 'keeper, pictured in vocal action in the 1971 F.A. Cup Final

lost, on aggregate, and went out of the European Champions Cup, convinced that we had indeed been robbed.

That game is a distant memory now, of course; just like the F.A. Cup quarter-final we played against Bolton Wanderers at Burnden Park, the year we beat Leeds at Wembley. But although I've scored more than 50 goals for Liverpool, the one I got at Bolton stands out in my mind, as well. For with only a minute or so left for play, I collected a cross from Peter Thompson which beat everyone, and as I raced in from the right I met the ball with my head, and popped it past Eddie Hopkinson, for the winner.

If that was the best goal I think I've ever scored, I'm certain about the worst miss of my career—for it was the one and only penalty I've

ever taken for Liverpool. That came in a game when we beat Arsenal 5-0 at Anfield, and facing us that day was our old goalkeeper, Jim Furnell. We didn't have a regular penalty taken—Tommy Smith usually does the job for us, these days—and I think, after Roger Hunt had missed two spot kicks on the trot, that the job was being handed around a bit. Anyway, it fell to me; and as I was about to hit the ball, I suddenly changed my mind. I'd been intending to place the shot, and then I started to think about blasting it . . . and I did neither. Jim Furnell saved it.

Today, Liverpool have a new-look team. Names such as Ron Yeats, Roger Hunt, Ian St. John and Tommy Lawrence have departed. Now the fans cheer players like Kevin Keegan, John Toshack and Steve Heighway. "The boss"

The always—well, nearly always—smiling Emlyn Hughes takes a tumble in a match against Wolves

decided a couple of seasons or so ago that the time had come to break up the old team, and try to win new glories with a new one. And we came pretty close to doing it, straight away. For in the first season of the "new" Liverpool, we went to Wembley in the F.A. Cup Final, and when Steve Heighway scored, we all thought we'd cracked it. But Arsenal came back and Charlie George popped in a goal which did the trick in extra time, to give Arsenal the League and Cup double.

Then we almost won the League, the following season, for we embarked on a tremendous run which took us through the second half of the season with barely a defeat. But at the finish, it was Derby County who pipped us for the title. Yet, Liverpool being Liverpool, we came again last season, as we put all our efforts

into trying to win some new honour. We were in the League race, we were in the running for the E.U.F.A. Cup and the F.A. Cup. And now we're going at it again.

People ask me what I think about the "new" team at Anfield, and I'm bound to say I think it will get better and better, and win as much honour as the team of the 1960's. As for me, I hope I can keep going for a few more seasons, and chalk up some more games. If you're wondering how I've kept going so long, I'll give you the answer in three little words. Dedication —and luck. I like to think I've been dedicated to making a success of my career; and I know I've been lucky in playing for such a great club and avoiding serious injury. Football is a job that demands dedication . . . and we all need some luck in our lives, don't we?

the SCOTTISH SCENE

A goal in the first minute for Glasgow Rangers as Sandy Jardine (in the dark shirt) beats Bayern Munich's international keeper Sepp Maier with a deceptive shot in the second leg of the 1972 European Cup Winners Cup semi-final. Rangers won 3-1 on aggregate and beat Moscow Dynamo 3-2 in the Final.

(Right) Back to Scottish domestic football—and the always fiercely contested matches between the Old Firm of Celtic and Rangers. George Connelly and Willie Johnston in a race for possession

This would make a good 'Spot the Ball' competition picture—except that the ball has been scrambled away with Kilmarnock's Eddie Morrison still airborne and Rangers' Colin Jackson 'saved by the post'—unless Eddie landed on him!

(Right) *Alan Gordon of Hibs and Ian Rennie of St. Johnstone in action*

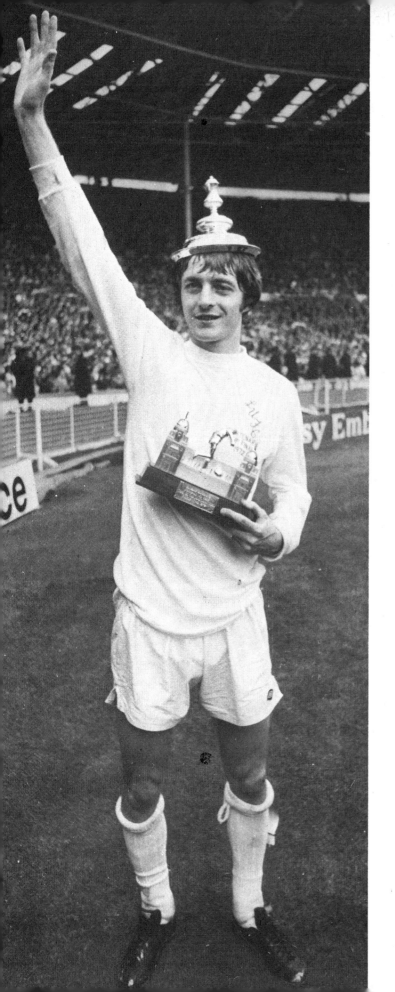

(Left) *Allan Clarke, crowned with the 'lid' of the 'pot', and holding his Man of the Match award after Leeds had beaten Arsenal in the 1972 F.A. Cup Final* (Right) *1969 F.A. Cup Final with Allan Clarke in action for Leicester against Manchester City's Neil Young who scored the only goal of the match*

I last wrote an article for **ALL STARS** five years ago. I was, at the time of writing it, a Fulham player and I wrote in my article that 'getting to a First Division club was always a burning ambition with me' from the time I first played football when I was at Shortheath Secondary Modern School.

I went on in that earlier article to tell you how I had seemed all set to join Aston Villa at the age of 14 as a ground-staff boy but then along came Bill Moore, then the manager of Walsall, to see me and Dad, and instead I reported to Fellows Park and started my football career, along with seven other ground-staff boys. My job was usually working in the dressing-room, getting the kit ready and cleaning the boots!

At seventeen I signed as a professional player with Walsall and five weeks later made my first team debut playing against Reading at home. I settled in the first team, scoring 23 league goals in the 1964-65 season, and held my place through changes of manager and chairman at Walsall. Then, soon after my eighteenth birthday, Vic Buckingham, then the manager of Fulham, started taking an interest in me and, after holding fire whilst Walsall progressed to the 4th Round of the F.A. Cup, I signed for the London club in March 1966.

Great Moments with LEEDS

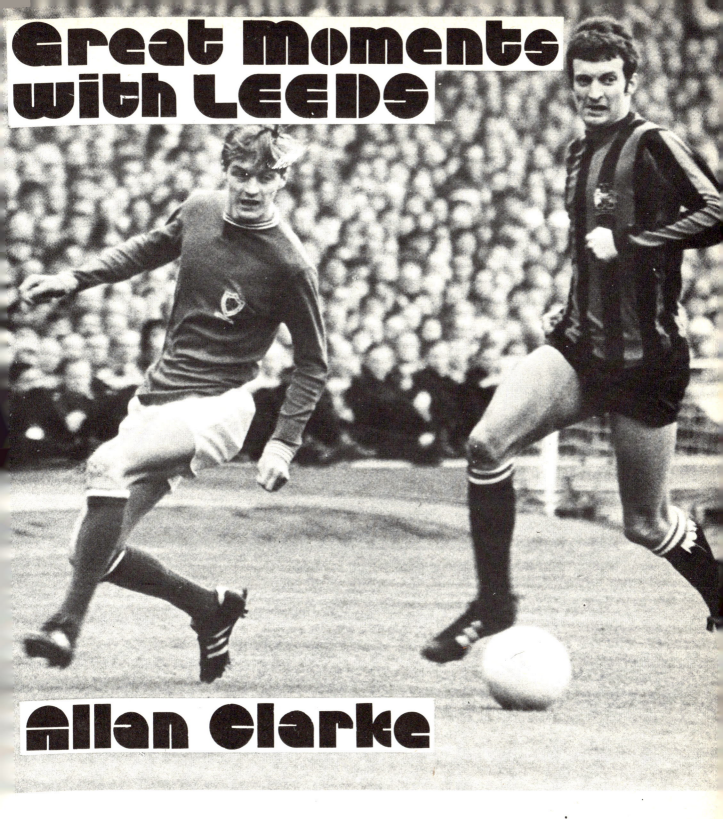

Allan Clarke

LEEDS ARE A TEAM OF GOOD, VERY GOOD, AND GREAT PLAYERS, EVERY ONE OF WHOM IS CAPABLE OF TURNING ON THOSE PATCHES OF UNEXPECTED, INSPIRED PLAY THAT CAN PRODUCE GOALS . . .

Fulham were then a First Division club and before the 1965-66 season ended I had played my first six matches in the First Division of the Football League. I suppose that what most football fans remember about 1966 is that it was the year in which England won the World Cup. A sadder recollection is that the two clubs relegated at the end of the 1965–66 season from the First Division were Northampton and Blackburn Rovers. Rovers, of course, are one of the great names of football–they had won the F.A. Cup three years in a row before the Football League had even been formed, but since dropping from the First in 1966 they have slipped a further rung down the ladder to the Third.

As for Northampton–there can never have been such a remarkable example of the ups-and-downs of football as Northampton's over the past twelve years: from the Fourth promoted to the Third at the end of the season 1960-61; from Third to Second (1962-63) and from Second to First (1964-65). Then, as I have mentioned, relegated from the First to the Second (1965-66)–and the downward journey from Second to Third (1966-67), from Third to Fourth (1968-69) and even, at the end of the 1971-72 season, having to apply for re-election to the Fourth Division!

That's not my story however. I was, as I wrote in that earlier article of mine, playing in the First Division with Fulham and making my first appearance for the England U-23 side (in October 1966 against Wales). My job was to score goals and I could feel reasonably pleased with 24 First Division goals for Fulham in my first full season with them, and four goals for the U-23's in that match against Wales. Goals were, it is worth noting, more plentiful in 1966-67 than they have been the past two or three seasons! For example, although Fulham finished 18th in the table, and Southampton (for whom Ron Davies scored 37 league goals) 19th, they scored 71 and 74 goals respectively. In 1971-72 Derby County won the championship with 69 goals, my present club Leeds were runners-up with 73, and the *highest* scorers in the First Division, Manchester City, scored 77. It's a harder job being a striker today!

At the end of the next season–that is to say,

a few months after I wrote that earlier article– Fulham were bottom but, as things happened, that did not mean that my experience of First Division football had been short-lived. Instead in June 1968, at the age of 21, I was transferred to Leicester City for what amounted to a £150,000 fee–it was partly an exchange deal that took Frank Large to Fulham. It was, incidentally, the last of three transfers in 1968 that involved the Clarke family–in February my elder brother Frank had been transferred from Shrewsbury to Queens Park Rangers, and in May younger brother Derek had joined Wolves from my first club Walsall.

So the season 1968-69 opened with Fulham in the Second Division but with me still playing the First Division–with Leicester City, and still keeping in touch with what I had written six months before in my article that 'I would really like an opportunity of going to Mexico in 1970 when England defend the World Cup.'

It was a disappointing season for Leicester City that saw Matt Gillies resign as manager and Frank O'Farrell take his place shortly before Christmas, the club relegated from the First Division (finishing just above Q.P.R.), and, to cap it all, being beaten in the F.A. Cup Final by Manchester City for whom Neil Young scored the only goal of the match. I suppose in the usual way of things, once the first sense of disappointment has worn off, the beaten finalists can get some consolation from remembering that they had got into the F.A. Cup Final at Wembley–and only two clubs do that each season!

In our case however even that consolation was reduced because we knew we were due for the Second Division the next season. For two of us however, Peter Shilton and myself, there was to be an England interlude when we went with the party who played matches in Mexico, Uruguay and Brazil as part of the preparations for the 1970 World Cup. And although I did not get a game in the team in a recognised Full international match I did play at Guadalajara for the England XI that beat the Mexican XI (that was their international team) by four goals to nil. Jack Charlton, Bobby Moore, Alan Ball, Colin Bell, and Martin Peters (for whom Bobby Charlton came on as sub.) were all in the England

1970 F.A. Cup Final: The disgraceful Wembley pitch after Leeds' two-all draw with Chelsea

team, and Jeff Astle and I shared the goals scored.

Then soon after the tour finished—in June 1969—I was on the move again: to Leeds for £165,000 that was again the highest transfer between two British clubs until Martin Peters went from West Ham to Spurs the following March.

Leeds had returned to the First Division for the season 64-65 after their second post-war spell in the Second Division, and had been in the top flight of clubs ever since. In 1968 they had won the Football League Cup and, early in the 1968-69 season the Fairs Cup Final held over from the previous May. Then, as Leicester were relegated and beaten in the Cup Final, Leeds had become the Football League champions for the

first time in their history.

That was the great club I was joining and I was soon, in that hectic 1969-70 season, involved in Leeds usual striving for the honours. In the end that season we had to be content with reaching the semi-final of the European Champions Cup (where we lost to Celtic), finishing second to Everton in the Football League, and—this was the biggest disappointment—losing to Chelsea in a replayed F.A. Cup Final at Old Trafford.

This was, of course, my second appearance in the Cup Final in successive years. We played some fine football on a Wembley pitch in rather a poor condition (the F.A. Year Book later described it as 'wet, patchy, and sanded . . . a disgrace'), took the lead after about a quarter of

1970 F.A. Cup Final: Allan Clarke eludes Tommy Baldwin's tackle—Paul Madeley in the background. Leeds were beaten 1-2 in the replayed Final at Old Trafford

an hour and generally controlled the play. Then just before half-time Chelsea equalised with a 'Cup-Final freak of a goal.' Again we took command in the second-half and when we scored with only six minutes to go no one was surprised. The surprise was when Chelsea equalised two minutes later.

Extra time brought no goals and, for the first time since 1912, the Cup Final had to be replayed. Again as in the first match we dominated the play for long periods and scored first. Let me again quote how the F.A. Year Book reported it:

'For all of the first half, and for a good part of the second, Leeds were quicker to the ball, covering better and passing more accurately, yet

Some consolation for Allan Clarke—two months after the 1970 F.A. Cup Final he made his debut for England in Guadalajara against Czechoslovakia in the World Cup—and scored the only goal of the match

twelve minutes from the end Chelsea equalised again.'

In the two matches we had led three times; each time Chelsea had pulled us back. Now the replay went to extra time and Chelsea went ahead for the first time—and stayed in front.

In many ways 1970 was the year of 'so near and yet so far' as, soon after the Cup Final, I joined the England World Cup squad. I played in one of the matches en route to Mexico but it was not a Full international and when I did make my first appearance for England in a Full international match it was in the World Cup itself. The match was against Czechoslovakia— the third and last of our matches in the first round, and one from which we needed to get at least one point to be certain of qualifying with

Brazil for the quarter-finals. Before the match, and in the knowledge that Geoff Hurst, who was then the penalty-taker, was not playing, Sir Alf Ramsey asked for volunteers to take any penalty. No one spoke at first so I offered to have a go. Our Leeds trainer, Les Cocker, was in on the discussion and Sir Alf turned enquiringly to him. But Johnny Giles was the Leeds' penalty-taker so Les had no experience of my capability for that job!

My approach to taking a penalty is simple. It offers a good chance of a goal—if it goes in. If it doesn't, it's a miss like any other.

Which is not to pretend that when I volunteered I expected that in my first Full international match and in the special atmosphere of the World Cup, I would have to take a penalty.

May 1971. Allan Clarke (right of picture) *scores for Leeds against the Italian club Juventus in the second leg (at Leeds) of the Fairs Cup Final. The aggregate score was 3-3 and Leeds' won with more away goals*

In fact I did and my goal from the spot was the only one scored in the match.

The next match in the World Cup was the quarter-final against West Germany in which, as had been expected, Francis Lee, Alan Ball and Bobby Charlton returned in place of Jeff Astle, Colin Bell and myself. There were still the semi-final and the final to come—but not, as things turned out, for us. For 70 minutes of that quarter-final England had the game under control and were leading by goals scored by Alan Mullery and Martin Peters in the 31st and 49th minutes. Then Beckenbauer scored with a speculative shot and nine minutes from time Uwe Seeler headed the equaliser. So to extra-time—and everyone thought of four years before when England had beaten West Germany 4-2 in extra time in the 1966 World Cup Final. This time in Mexico it was West Germany who won—3-2.

The next season (1970-71) I missed only one league match for Leeds. Once again we finished

in second place—to Arsenal who did the Cup and League 'double'. Our own F.A. Cup campaign had been stopped by Colchester, but late in May and early in June 1971 we won the two-legged Fairs Cup (the last time that competition was staged. It has been replaced by the U.E.F.A. Cup competition). And shortly before those Fairs Cup Final matches I had played for England against Malta and Northern Ireland. In those matches, as in one against East Germany the previous November, I had scored to make my personal record—four appearances, four goals.

In the season 1971-72 for the third season in succession Leeds finished in second place in the Football League championship. We might have done better even than that except for having to play too many vital matches in too few days at the end of the season. People not very closely involved in football often argue that professional footballers trained to peak fitness ought to be able to play two or three matches every week

March 1972–a First Division match against West Ham in London. Paul Reaney, Billy Bonds and Allan Clarke (on defensive duty) in action

1972 F.A. Cup Final: Third time lucky for Allan Clarke (out of picture) *who has just headed the only goal of the match against Arsenal. The ball in the net; Arsenal's keeper Geoff Barnett on his knees–and Leeds' joyful No. 6 is Norman Hunter*

without much effect. What they forget–or never even begin to understand–is that it is time between matches that is needed to maintain fitness. As the end of a season approaches with any successful club engaged in the race for the championship, in the F.A. Cup competition and probably in a European competition also, the constant endeavour is to get enough players fit for each match.

In the 1971-72 season Leeds, from the middle of April to Monday, 8 May, had to play a semi-final and the Final of the F.A. Cup and four vital league matches. We gained four points from those four matches: five points would have given us the championship. But there was consolation in that we won the Cup when I headed the only goal of the match against Arsenal at Wembley.

It was my third F.A. Cup Final in four seasons–and the first victorious one. It was for all of us at Leeds some return for the one that had got away two years before, and it was the more deserved because we knew that several of us on the field were nursing injuries that in mid-season would have meant taking a rest.

For me, 6 May 1972: Leeds 1 Arsenal 0 in the F.A. Cup Final at Wembley is my finest football moment to date–but I am hoping for others to match it both in the Leeds and in the England strip.

What is it that makes Leeds such a great side and one able to maintain a high standard from season to season? The answer is simple. Leeds are a team who play as a team with every player prepared to run his heart out for each other. Any club with players like that will do well but

Two determined 'red heads'—Alan Ball (Arsenal) and Leeds' skipper Billy Bremner in a duel in the pouring rain!

Leeds are also a team of good, very good, and great players, every one of whom is capable of turning on those patches of unexpected, inspired play that can produce goals or the chances for someone else to score.

It is great to be part of the Leeds squad and I am looking forward to sharing in several more great moments with the club.

And with England? I have been attending England squad training 'get-togethers' since 1966. I remember how nervous I felt when I reported for the first time but that soon passed in the happy atmosphere that always develops. I had, as I have mentioned, to wait until the World Cup in Mexico in 1970 before I made my first appearance in a Full international match but that does not mean that I had four years of disappointed waiting.

On the contrary, setting aside appearance for the U-23s, the Football League and the England XI, my personal experience is that I have always come away from an England 'club' get-together feeling ever more determined to work at my own game.

The only disappointment is that pressure of fixtures and the need to balance the needs of clubs, who do after all employ the players and pay the wages, and the national squad not only limits the number of national team training spells that can be arranged, it also does often players attending because of club commitments.

Johnny Giles' delight at winning a F.A. Cup winners medal is shared by his son (right) *and his brother-in-law's son – and his brother-in-law is Nobby Stiles*

FOOTBALL····
THE UNIVERSAL GAME
How it all began
by Gordon Jeffery

Ball games existed from the beginning of recorded history—and probably before then. In some the ball was thrown, in others it was hit, and in others it was kicked. How and when the games were played varied from one part of the world to another, and from one part of a region or country to another part of the same country. Climatic conditions that have done so much to condition national character and temperament clearly influenced the nature of the games played. Generally the colder the climate, the more robust and energetic were the games played.

An energetic, boisterous, kicking, physical game like football had been played in England for hundreds of years before the game as we know it today became established. It was a game that appealed to the common people more than to their lords and masters who on several occasions sought to outlaw football. Both King Edward in 1314 and King Richard in 1389, for examples, passed Acts banning the game—on the pretext that many evils and great noise were caused by 'hustling over large balls' but really because they wanted their subjects to engage in sports like archery which would be useful in time of war.

The prohibitions did not stop people from kicking the ball. Nor, two hundred years later, in Tudor England, did complaints that football 'causeth necks, legs, backs and arms to be broken, eyes to start out, and noses to gush with blood,' or that playing the game engendered 'envy, malice, rancour, choler, hatred, displeasure, enmity, and what not else.'

Stubbes, the English sixteenth-century writer, in his *Anatomie of Abuses* accused football of 'causing,' in addition to 'fighting, brawling, contention, quarrel picking, and great effusion of blood,' '*murder* and *homicide*' 'as *daily* experience teacheth.' (My italics: he was I think, perhaps exaggerating.)

The Industrial Revolution in Britain influenced the sports and pastimes of the people as, of course, it influenced their lives as a whole. The considerable movement of people from villages to the growing towns, and the extremely long hours worked in the new factories by men, women and even children, limited the time, place and opportunity for taking part in the traditional sports and pastimes. Many died out or were played, or have since been revived, by only a small sector of the population where previously they had been enjoyed by the entire village community.

Football survived, and particularly in the Public Schools. It was played however in a different way in almost every different school with some, as Rugby for example, allowing players not only to pick up the ball but to run with it. Other schools who allowed a measure of handling the ball, limited the use of the hand to stopping the ball and then dropping it to the foot.

The different sets of rules in different schools

Football the Universal Game: A Soviet First Division match between CSKA Moscow (the Army club) and Wings of the Soviet Kuibeshev (the Air Force club), at the splendid Lenin Stadium in Moscow

—usually unwritten rules passed on from one group of boys to newcomers, made it almost impossible for matches to be contested between different schools. It also led to confusion when boys from the different schools came together at Oxford or Cambridge University and wanted to play a game of football. And it was at Cambridge that the first effective moves were made towards drawing up a uniform set of rules. These first discussions had only a limited influence but they pointed the way and on 26 October 1863 – the first important date in football's history – a meeting was held in London that agreed to the formation of The Football Association. And that, incidentally, remains to this day the name of the Association that controls the game in England without mention of the name of the country.

Only eleven clubs had representatives at that first meeting – all were from the London area, and all were enrolled as original members once the motion that 'the clubs represented at this meeting now form themselves into an association to be called "*The Football Association*"' had been resolved unanimously.

None of the Public Schools at which the game was played were represented although the Charterhouse captain was amongst a number of 'interested persons' at the meeting. Nor was there as yet any contact with those responsible for the organisation of the game in provincial areas like Sheffield (where a football club had been formed in 1855), Lincoln and Stoke. More years were to pass before the rules drawn up by The Football Association were to be generally accepted by all who played the game in the United Kingdom.

Yet from the very beginning the founder members in drawing up the set of rules declared their intention to be the removal of the barriers

Football the Universal Game: The Brazilian club, Santos, attacking against Portugal's Benfica in a match played in Rio. Pelé is the white-shirted player challenging the keeper, Costa Pereira

that prevented 'the accomplishment of one universal game.'

It is doubtful if any of those present at the meeting at the Freemasons' Tavern in October 1963 realised how truly universal the game would become once those barriers were removed.

The advantages of a generally accepted set of rules were many. There was the obvious one that the Public Schools could now play matches against each other instead of merely between teams in their own schools. There was the almost as obvious one that as many of the boys left school for colleges at Cambridge and Oxford Universities they could carry on playing without needing to learn any variation of rules.

More important than these however was the fact that now, as those who had learned to play the game under the uniform code of rules left school or university and joined, or, as was more often the case, *formed* football clubs, they were able to spread the rules—the same rules. Many of these new clubs were outside of London. The industrialisation of Britain had stabilised to some extent. The new trade unions and parliamentary legislation had reduced the long working hours in the factories, and improved conditions. There was now some time for leisure pursuits; to play games—and to watch them. And it was football, above all games, that working people in the industrial areas were seeking. As G.M. Young the social historian noted in his collection of essays *Early Victorian England*:

'The upper and middle classes in the shape of the schools borrowed the game from the people, and in the end, the people took their own game back again.'

The most important single factor in the spread in scope of the game and, of course, the spread of influence of the Football Association,

Football the Universal Game. In an international match at Reykjavik, Bermuda are defending against the home side, Iceland

was the introduction of the F.A. Cup competition in 1872—the first football competition in the world. Only 15 clubs entered for the first competition—eight of them from the London area. Only two of the clubs have remained in existence: Maidenhead and the Scottish club Queen's Park. Maidenhead, who have since amalgamated with another Maidenhead club, are the only club to have entered for every competition for the F.A. Cup since its inception.

The first Cup Final played at Kennington Oval on 16 March 1872 attracted two thousand people and was won by Wanderers who defeated Royal Engineers by one goal to nil. Wanderers, Oxford University, Royal Engineers, Old Etonians, Clapham Rovers, and Old Carthusians won the first eleven competitions for the F.A. Cup: Wanderers themselves taking five of them, three in a row between 1876 and 1878 which entitled them to retain the trophy. Instead they handed it back on the understanding that it must always remain the property of the Football Association.

The first strong challenge to the domination of the competition by these senior London and near London club came in 1882 when Old

Etonians met a club called Blackburn Rovers in the Cup Final. The attendance was 7,000—the largest attendance yet at a Cup Final and some of the increase in the attendance must have been due to the curiosity of Londoners about these invaders from the north. Amongst the Blackburn side incidentally was a Scotsman named Fergus Suter. Some years before Suter and his friend James Love were members of a club called Partick Glasgow, one of a number of Scottish clubs that occasionally came south to play against clubs in Yorkshire and Lancashire which were springing up like mushrooms almost overnight.

Love first, and later his friend Suter, decided that they liked the look of things south of the border where wages in industry seemed to be higher. But there is no doubt whatsoever that they found it possible to secure employment in Darwen, Lancashire, as much, if not more, because of their ability as footballers than for any other reason. Not yet perhaps were they professional footballers in the sense that the money they received for playing for Darwen was the main source of their livelihood. But it was because they could play football well that they were employed in the little town that in 1879 became the first provincial, northern club to really disturb the complacency of the London and southern clubs.

Darwen, with a team consisting largely of lads working in the mills of the little town, had a walkover in the First Round and an easy 4-1 win over a Lancashire village side in the Second Round before being drawn against Remnants, a London based team of old Public School boys who won the toss for choice of ground and elected to play at Slough. Darwen won by the odd goal of five to reach the Fourth Round—that was, in fact, half a step beyond the quarter-final stage since six clubs were involved, with the winners of one of the Fourth Round matches certain of a bye direct to the Final!

In the semi-final Darwen were drawn against the Old Etonians at the Oval (the venue for the Cup Finals at the time). The cost of another journey south was beyond the funds of the club but the townspeople of Darwen found the money for their lads to challenge the Old Etonians. At half-time the score was 4-0 in favour of the Old Etonians. Soon after the interval Darwen found themselves five goals in arrears and although they scored once themselves, the score was still 5-1 for the home side with a quarter of an hour left for play. Then, as ever since, fitba' has been a funny game and Darwen scored four times in those last fifteen minutes to end the ninety minutes all square.

More than that, it was the Old Etonians who declined to play extra time. This was doubly inconsiderate since there was then no provision for the venue to be changed when a Cup match was drawn. Instead Darwen had again to face the cost and the tedium of the long journey to London for the replay. Again a Darwen subscription was opened to which the Football Association gave £10 and the Old Etonians £5. So three weeks later the Lancashire lads returned to the Oval and again the match was drawn—two-all. A week later the by now somewhat bemused Darwen players came south again but this time they were defeated by six goals to two.

Darwen's three matches against the Old Etonians had focussed considerable sporting attention on the little club. In the meantime however successive victories over the Old Harrovians (2-0) and Oxford University (2-1) had taken another provincial club, Nottingham Forest, a stage further than Darwen—to the semi-final where they lost to the Old Etonians. Two years later Darwen themselves, after beating Sheffield Wednesday 5-1 and Romford 15-0, reached the semi-final before being beaten by the Old Carthusians 4-1.

So to the next year, 1882, and the first appearance of a provincial club in the Final—Blackburn Rovers with, as I have written, Fergus Suter, once of Darwen, in their team. Blackburn Rovers valued him greatly and a Lancashire paper reported that 'rather than let Darwen reclaim Suter, the Blackburn Rovers had arranged to pay him £100 for his services'. That was, of course, in the days before professionalism was seen to be in existence.

Blackburn Rovers failed to win the Final of 1882 but just one year later another Blackburn club, Blackburn Olympic, beat Old Etonians (making their third successive appearance) in the Final. The Old Etonians side bristled with international players including the legendary Hon. A.F. Kinnaird. They were in every way typical of the 'old boys' who had got together and formed the Football Association twenty years before, and so made possible the F.A. Cup competition, the accomplishment of the universal game—and thus the appearance of the Blackburn Olympic team in London in a Cup Final.

The Olympic team was made up of players from a wider range of occupations than any previous winners of the Cup. Their captain, Warburton, was a master plumber. Others were an iron moulder, a spinner, a picture framer, a dentist's assistant and a cotton mill operative. Two were weavers—and, significantly, two seemed to follow no occupation, except playing football.

The game that the upper and middle classes had borrowed had been re-claimed by the ordinary people—not exclusively but effectively. Geoffrey Green in his *History of the F.A. Cup* relates a story that the streets of Blackburn were thronged with waving crowds as, in a wagonette drawn by six horses, and accompanied by brass bands, the Olympic team came home in triumph. Warburton held the Cup aloft for the townspeople to see the trophy they had read about, heard about but never seen before. Somebody in the crowd shouted his disappointment at the appearance of the Cup, suggesting it only looked like a tea kettle. 'Ey, lad' agreed Warburton, 'but it's very welcome to Lancashire; it'll have a good home and it'll ne'er go back to Lunnon.'

As a matter of fact that particular trophy never did. In 1895 it was stolen from the shop window of a football and football boot manufacturer in Birmingham—the Cup then being held by Aston Villa, and it was never recovered. That nicety apart, it was many years before a London club did again win the Cup after, in 1883, Blackburn Olympic had taken it away from the capital. Blackburn Rovers three times in succession; Aston Villa, West Bromwich Albion; Preston North End, Blackburn Rovers twice in succession; West Bromwich Albion

again, Wolverhampton Wanderers; Notts County, Aston Villa again; Sheffield Wednesday; Aston Villa yet again; Nottingham Forest; Sheffield United; and Bury all got their names inscribed as winners before, in 1901, Tottenham Hotspur brought the Cup south again.

So football moved into the twentieth century. In a mere forty years the game of the old boys of the Public Schools of England who had formed the Football Association had conquered the whole of Britain. It had already taken root in several European countries and some in South America.

Today more than 130 different countries are in membership of the world's football organization, F.I.F.A.—98 of them entered for the 1974 World Championship.

In 1863 it had seemed such a little thing—to reach agreement on a set of rules. Truly that had removed the barriers to the accomplishment of the universal game.

Football the Universal Game: In 1971 Wembley, venue for the F.A. Cup Final since 1923, stages another Final—between Panathinaikos of Greece (dark shirts) and Ajax of the Netherlands for the European Champions Cup. Ajax won 2-0

YOU'VE GOT TO FIGHT BACK
by Joe Royle

A flying header from Joe Royle playing against Leeds last season

... YOU HAVE TO LEARN TO TAKE THE ROUGH WITH THE SMOOTH—AND YOU'VE ALWAYS GOT TO BE PREPARED TO COME FIGHTING BACK

If football has taught me one thing, it's that you can never afford to take anything for granted—and that there is always a need for you to be prepared to fight back. I'm not referring to tough stuff on the field; I'm talking about the ups and downs the game can bring... and I reckon I have had my fair share of them.

The first medals I ever collected came quite a few years ago—when I was aged seven or eight and played for Ranworth Square County Primary School. In the same season, I won a knock-out Cup medal and a league medal. Little did I dream that I would go on to play First Division football with Everton, and international football for England.

However, it's not all plain sailing in soccer, as I soon discovered for myself. I had barely become a teenage footballer, with visions of making a name for myself in the Liverpool Boys' side, when I 'copped it' in a tackle during a school match—and broke my left leg. At the time, I thought it was the end . . . but inside three months, I had recovered, and was back in action. Shortly afterwards, I claimed a place in the Liverpool Boys team; and to me, at the time, it was almost like playing for England.

I progressed to the point where I was chosen as skipper of the Lancashire side, and then I was invited to go along and show what I could do as an England Schoolboy trialist. Once again, I came up against a stumbling block on the road to soccer success— I couldn't take part, because of school football commitments. But it wasn't the end of the world, for a few months later I was asked if I fancied signing for Everton. When I played for Lancashire against Cheshire, I was pleased enough to have scored, although we lost 2-1; I often wonder whether I'd have scored more—or muffed the one I got—had I known that Everton manager Harry Catterick was watching me!

When I had left school, and spent an hour with the Everton boss, and seen the set-up at Goodison, there was no hesitation about it—I signed on the dotted line, and set out on the trail of success or failure as a would-be professional footballer. Then came another jolt—I discovered that as an apprentice footballer, I didn't just play in a match and shoot off home . . . there was the kit to be cleared away, and we had to wash the dressing-room floors.

They made me work at my game, too—sometimes I felt that I was being really pushed. But the pay-off came when the manager told me that I would be playing in a First Division game at Blackpool. I was still an apprentice, still a lad with a lot to learn—but what a tremendous vote of confidence that was, for someone who was only 16. I'd like to say that we won; but, again,

I learned that football has its ups and down, for we lost, 2-0, and I knew that I had failed to shine. Still, I got another first-team chance that season. And two years later, I was walking out on the Wembley turf to play in Everton's F.A. Cup Final side against West Brom.

It's history now that Everton lost in extra time, because Jeff Astle scored the only goal of the game, for West Brom. We were choked with disappointment, but we had to learn to grin and bear it. You can take it from me that there is very little worse in big-time football than going to the F.A. Cup Final full of hope, and finishing up collecting a loser's medal.

But even so, there ARE one or two things which can eclipse such a shattering disappointment, as I discovered later in my career. In 1966, Everton had been to Wembley and won the Cup, against Sheffield Wednesday; in 1968, when I was in the side, we had lost to West Brom . . . and I wondered why I couldn't have been in a winning side. But in 1971, my hopes were revived, because we were going well . . . and I had just collected a medal as a member of Everton's Football League Championship winning team.

After that fabulous season when we overhauled Leeds United to carry off the title, everyone at Goodison thought that this was the start of a real assault on all the honours that were going—and that included the European Champions Cup. But fickle fortune had one or two tricks to play, and the bottom just about fell out of our world in a few days.

First of all, we came up against a Greek team called Panathinaikos, in the European Champions Cup. They were managed by Ferenc Puskas, who starred in a great Hungarian victory over England years ago, and had been a great player with Real Madrid. At Goodison, we were shaken when the Greeks snatched a goal, and we only just managed to draw the first leg on our own ground. In the return game, which was a really tough, bruising affair, we held Panathinaikos—but they went into the next round because of the goal they had scored at Goodison Park. So that was the end of our dreams of a place in the European Champions Cup Final.

We returned to England to try to pick up the pieces, and for me, at least, there was one bit of

1968 F.A. Cup Final—and a disappointment for young Joe Royle (left of picture) *playing for Everton against West Bromwich Albion for whom Jeff Astle* (third from left) *scored the only goal*

good news. My wife, Janet, presented me with a son. The following day, it was back to the soccer action, for we were in the semi-finals of the F.A. Cup, and we were determined to gain some consolation for our defeat in Greece. Especially as our opponents were our greatest rivals, Liverpool.

The semi-final was staged at Old Trafford, and we scored first. We were right on top, and looked like cruising into the final. But tragedy struck, when centre-half Brian Labone received

an injury which forced him to hobble off the field, and Liverpool, who never seem to know when they're beaten, struck back not only to equalise, but to snatch a winner.

I can still remember how I felt, as I walked off the Old Trafford pitch. It was as though I and my team-mates had slogged ourselves to death virtually through the season, only to see what we had built come crumbling down at the end, in that fateful week. Within the space of a few days, we had been bundled out of the

Another reminder of the 1968 Final with Joe Royle challenging John Osborne

Joe Royle and Martin Chivers in action for England against Malta–Joe Royle's debut for England in a Full international match

European Champions Cup, and had seen Liverpool snatch the prize of going to Wembley from our grasp. Not surprisingly, there were a few Everton players almost in tears, as they slumped dejectedly on to the seats in the Old Trafford dressing-room. As we filed out, afterwards, people patted us on the shoulder and smiled sympathetically, as they said: 'Hard luck . . .' But there just didn't seem to be any sort of consolation for us.

Once again, it appeared to be the end of the world. But once again, we learned that you cannot sit around moping and feeling sorry for yourself. There were still some matches to be played, before the season was over. And play them we did, even if we felt that for us, the season had ended the week that Panathinaikos and Liverpool had beaten us.

I expect by now that you're really beginning to appreciate what I said about the ups and

downs of soccer. As I told you, I've certainly experienced both sides.

Two seasons ago, nothing seemed to go right for Everton, and I was one of the players who went through a lean spell. Things got to the stage where I didn't seem to be able to stick the ball into the back of the net—and I'd been averaging almost a goal every other game, right through my career—and so it came as no real surprise when I was dropped from the first team. My one great memory of that season is the day we thrashed Southampton at Goodison Park. We scored eight goals—and I thumped home four of them. That was the third hat-trick of my career. One was against Leicester City and the other one, oddly enough, was against Southampton in a previous match.

Last season, we set out determined to show that Everton could come good again, and after seven games, I'd got half a dozen goals under my belt, and I was going like a house on fire. I had also made my second appearance for England in a full international, to add to the half-dozen caps I'd collected at Under-23 level. The full international was against Yugoslavia, and people were good enough to praise my performance, and start tipping me to land a place in England's 1974 World Cup squad.

Then came more trouble. The back injury which had plagued me for much of the previous season returned—and it was worse than ever. After those seven League games and the England outing, I was out of action completely for weeks on end. I had a spell of rest in hospital, I started training, only for the back to go again. Finally, the matter was diagnosed as a slipped disc, and I can tell you it was agony for me to try to run, on occasions, never mind play competitive football. Even walking was a bit of a strain, at times.

Naturally, I became very worried about the situation, and the club was rather concerned. So much so, that it was arranged for me to fly up to Scotland to see a specialist there. I made two trips, and for a time I thought that I might just be able to get back into First Division action within a few weeks. But, eventually, I had to go into hospital—and the verdict was that I wouldn't play again for the rest of the season.

So, once again, I learned a lesson, during those long weeks of inactivity, and that was to be patient and keep on hoping that I could get back into my stride—especially on a football pitch. You won't be surprised when I say that I couldn't wait to see the end of 1972, and I fervently hoped that 1973 would bring me much better luck.

But the main thing, as I have stressed right through this article, is that you have to learn to take the rough with the smooth—and you've always got to be prepared to come fighting back, whether it's against injury, loss of form, or your opponents on a Saturday afternoon. So long as you realise this, then you'll keep going. And I hope that's what YOU are determined to do!

England v Yugoslavia, October 1972: Joe Royle's flying header beats the Yugoslav keeper Maric. Mike Channon also in the picture

DOES ONE MAN MAKE A TEAM?

asks HARRY STANLEY

The genius of George Best seen here scoring for Manchester United in a Cup match despite the proximity of five Stoke players—including Gordon Banks

I'LL ALWAYS ARGUE THAT WHEN YOU'VE GOT A GENIUS, THERE IS ONLY ONE WAY TO LET HIM PLAY—FREE AND UNFETTERED

Does one man make a team?—That's a question which is almost guaranteed to set people arguing, even though most of them will start out by saying fervently: "No one footballer EVER made a team!" But, on reflection, some of the people who dismiss the "one-man band" idea will start to think ... of players like Bryan Douglas, Tom Finney, Stanley Matthews and—inevitably—George Best.

Douglas was the man who came inside from the right wing, and made Blackburn Rovers tick in the days—not so long ago, at that—when they were still a First Division force. Douglas was no giant; he played his football with a poker-faced attitude, though, that let his deeds do the talking for him, as he wove a way past defenders and teed up scoring chances for snipers like Derek Dougan, Peter Dobing and Roy Vernon.

Dougan moved on, finally to win general—and genuine—acclaim with Wolves; Dobing was transferred to Manchester City, and then became captain and a midfield master for Stoke; Vernon joined glamour-club Everton, before moving on to Stoke, too. Douglas?—He stayed at Blackburn, as did his former England team-mate, Ronnie Clayton. Perhaps, had "Duggie" moved earlier in his career, he would have been an even bigger name.

The one great thing about Douglas was that whenever he got the ball, people sensed that they were in for a spot of entertainment. And, in those days, that counted for a lot. "Duggie" didn't always win his battles against defenders, but he was a genuine ball-playing artist who could carve up defences and set a game alight with his flowing skill.

The same could be said about Tom Finney, the peerless prince of Preston, and Stanley Matthews, the wizard of dribble with Stoke City, Blackpool, and Stoke City once more. All of them were key men in the team; all of them were entertainers supreme. And, were they playing today, and in their prime, each of them would cost more than the £250,000 Derby County splashed on David Nish. Don't take just my word for this, either: simply ask your Dad.

Douglas, Finney and Matthews were THE artists in their respective teams. Much as George Best has been regarded as THE man to watch and savour with Manchester United, these past seasons. If you talk to players, most of them will tell you that they don't really want to be compared with other stars of a past era. They will say comparisons cannot be made—people tried to do this with Finney and Matthews, when both were playing—and they are right.

Finney was a player who, like Douglas, could take on and beat defenders. He looked almost frail, a pale, ghost-like footballer whose courage belied his apparent lack of brawn. It was wrong to compare him with Matthews, because they were different, even though they were alike. Douglas, Finney and Matthews were all alike, in that they had uncanny ability to beat opponents; Douglas, Finney and Matthews were alike, in that they were all wing men. But after that . . . each had his separate talents.

Douglas and Finney proved that they could move inside, while Matthews always did his damage from the wing. Finney also proved that he could play in any forward position—and score goals.

So, although the three masters were alike, they WERE different, and possibly it is true to say that of the three, Finney was the most complete all-round player. Just as George Best is the most complete all-round player of modern football.

Best has been described as a genius in football boots, and that description is not far off the mark. In the first half of last season before the "revolution" at Old Trafford, he played in a struggling side, and—for me—he was striving consciously to play a real team game. That is to Best's credit. But, perhaps surprisingly, I felt that the very fact that he was playing a controlled team game meant that, too often, we did not see the best of Best. He was subdued, restrained . . . the flashes of genius were restricted.

George has been in the limelight for several years now, and sometimes the publicity has been less than good. But forget, for a moment his off-the-field headline performances, and think about him simply as a star footballer. The previous season, you may remember, when United were top of the halfway stage, this was due largely to goals scored by George Best that probably no other player could have scored. Even then, people were apt to complain that George Best tried too often to be a one-man team; that he sought to beat more opponents than he should have done; that he held on to the ball when team-mates were in better positions to do damage—had they received the pass that never came.

I'll always argue that when you've got a genius, there is only one way to let him play— free and unfettered. Sure, he holds the ball too long, at times. Sure, he tries to beat too many defenders, at times. Sure, he loses the ball because of this, at times. But surely, also, his remarkable instinct for doing—and being able to do—the unorthodox, the unexpected (such as beating four men AND the goalkeeper, and backheeling the ball into the net) makes him a footballer apart.

This, I felt last season, was what Manchester

Ted MacDougall (dark shorts) in action for Bournemouth against Brighton before his transfer to Manchester United

United lost when George Best was being asked to play the team game. This instinctive, uncanny ability to turn a game and win it on his own was rejected to his, and United's, cost.

Those who claimed that George Best tried to be a team on his own, at times, were right—and wrong. Right, because he WAS keeping the ball to himself, when team-mates were waiting for the pass; wrong, because he WAS the one man who could often get away with it all and fox the opposition, as well as his own team-mates, to finish up by scoring a glorious, spectacular goal

(and one which, often enough, won the game).

Which brings us back to the original question: does one man make a team?—You have instances in the past few seasons of players who emerged as superstars with their respective clubs, stealing the headlines with almost monotonous regularity. Names which spring to mind are Rodney Marsh, the darling of Queen's Park Rangers fans; Ted MacDougall, the striker who took Bournemouth to within an ace of promotion two seasons ago; Malcolm Macdonald, the striker whom all the scouts trekked to see, when he was

Malcolm Macdonald (white shirt) in action for Luton against Sheffield United's Eddie Colquhoun. (Right) Macdonald in Newcastle's famous black-and-white striped shirt in similar heading action—this time against Arsenal's Jeff Blockley

hammering 'em home for Luton Town.

Many people would have claimed, at the time, that each of these players was a one-man team, that each was irreplaceable at his club. But Marsh went to Manchester City, MacDougall went to Manchester United, and Macdonald went to Newcastle United. And Rangers, Bournemouth and Luton didn't fade away and die . . .

Football, of course, IS so much a matter of opinion. Many people considered that had Gordon Banks been keeping goal in Mexico in

1970, England would never have surrendered their two-goal lead to West Germany. They reckoned, also, that Banks—acclaimed the world's greatest goalkeeper—was the man who inspired Stoke City to Wembley and their first-ever trophy, when they won the Football League Cup in March, 1972. Banks saved a penalty from Geoff Hurst on the way, and it made headlines, just as his "miracle" save from Pelé made headlines a few seasons ago.

Last season, Stoke struggled, despite their new signings up front. Bank spent a lot of time

out of action through injury, even before that car-crash accident which stunned football. A lot of folk reckoned that Stoke had struggled, mainly because they hadn't had their formidable last line of defence to give the other players confidence, and make saves which only he could make.

But—and I've said that football IS a matter of opinion—in my view, one man DOESN'T make a team. Not even George Best. If one man DID make a team, there would be no need for the other 10 players to turn up . . .

At the same time, I have no doubt at all that one man can play a MAJOR part in making a team. And, for my money, Douglas, Finney, Matthews, Banks and Best have been such footballers. For on them has rested more responsibility than on other individuals. From them has been expected more than from other individuals. And, by and large, all these players have lived up to the great expectations of the people who

went to see them play . . . and entertain.

I see almost as many football matches as a successful side such as Liverpool play in a season. And I know that the style of the game has changed, with the emphasis more on work-rate and teamwork, as against the old, more free-and-easy dependence upon individual brilliance and flair. But, good old days or bad new days (depending on which way you look at things), I STILL don't think that any one man MADE a team.

A few of them came pretty close to it; but they all need ten others to help them achieve what they did achieve. And, no matter how long the argument goes on, that's the way it will always be, in football. Some players ARE more gifted than others, and it shows on the field of play; but football remains essentially a team game, even though it has its stars. Right, then . . . anyone want to start the argument going again?

ALL STARS Picture Spotlight on BOBBY MOORE

There could not be a more appropriate time to turn our spotlight on Bobby Moore. It is as certain as anything can be in the world of football, that it is upon him more than any other single *player* that England's qualification for a place in the 1974 World Cup will depend. It is upon him that the responsibility for leading England on the field in those final matches in West Germany will rest.

But dependability and the acceptance of responsibility are so much taken for granted in Bobby Moore that his consistent greatness as a player has not perhaps always been recognised. With such a player as Bobby Moore his rare mistakes are noticed more than his sure tackling, his sharp interceptions and his imaginative distribution. For both his only club, West Ham United, and England he has been a captain, as well as a player, whose duties were not limited to calling when the referee tossed the coin. He showed his aptitude for leadership in the England Youth team in 1958—the same year that he made his first appearances in League football for West Ham.

He was 'called up' rather late in time to join England's squad for the 1962 World Cup matches in Chile; hustled through his vaccinations and the rest of the departure drill and pushed into his first appearance for England in a Full international match against Peru—the only 'warming-up' match played in South America before the World Cup matches. Moore made such an impressive debut that he kept his place for the World Cup matches.

From the time he made his first appearance to the end of the 1971-72 season, Bobby Moore had played in 95 of the 106 Full international matches played by England—and captained the national team regularly since May 1964.

His greatest moment was to collect the World Cup in 1966. It will be fitting to mark ten years as Captain of England by collecting it again in 1974.

(Above) *May 1964–Bobby Moore proudly displays the FA Cup after West Ham's victory in the Final over Preston North End. A year later, also at Wembley, he collected the European Cup Winners Cup when West Ham beat TSV Munich in the Final; and one further year later, and again at Wembley, Bobby Moore collected the Jules Rimet trophy after England's victory in the 1966 World Cup.*

(Opposite) *The youthful Bobby Moore in action for England against Bulgaria in Rancagua in the 1962 World Cup*

(Above) *Bobby Moore at home with his charming wife, Tina, who has helped him considerably in his career and in his business interests that, in his case, have never complicated his position as captain of West Ham AND* (opposite) *OF ENGLAND—leading his team out to play against Scotland at Wembley.*

Rodney Marsh's England and Manchester City team-mate, Colin Bell (No. 8), being chased by Chelsea's Alan Hudson

ROADS TO THE TOP
Rodney Marsh

SOON AFTER I ARRIVED I ADMITTED THAT IT WAS GOING TO BE GREAT PLAYING IN CITY'S TEAM

Rodney Marsh, late of QPR, makes his first appearance for Manchester City in March 1972

All roads, it was said in the days of the great Roman Empire, lead to Rome—and if not all, at least many, roads lead to the top in football. If you want me to name a place it would be I suppose—all roads lead to Wembley and wearing the England shirt there.

The road that seems at first glance to be the easiest to travel is to be spotted when a school-boy by a top club and engaged by them as an apprentice. (Until fairly recently, of course, it was to be taken on the ground staff—making the tea, seeing to the kit, and doing other menial jobs around the ground whilst learning to be a footballer—and learning is the right word.)

In the youth team (with maybe appearances in England's youth team) and then in the reserves and so on to the first team. That's a straightforward route with few diversions or excursions down cul de sacs but it is not always so straightforward as it seemed that it would be at the age of fifteen. Between then and signing as a fully fledged professional (at the age of seventeen) and getting a regular place in the first team a lot can happen in the world of football. A boy joining Ipswich in 1962 when they were the Football League champions would have been with a Second Division club when he was nineteen. A boy joining Second Division Derby County in 1968 would have been with the Football League *champions* four years later.

Nor, assuming that the top club is one that stays in and around the top the way that clubs like Arsenal, Liverpool, Leeds and Tottenham have done over the past ten years or so, is that straightforward route to the top necessarily the easiest one to travel. For one thing it is more crowded with other likely lads and although, on the surface, competition between players should produce the best from each of them, that does not always work out with youngsters, some of whom may shine brightly but then flicker out whilst others maintain a steady glow. The familiar story in the world of education of the late developer is also true of hopeful footballers.

It is naturally the bigger centres of population and of football interest that attract the hopeful footballers—London and the North West. For many years in the North West it was Manchester United who seemed to get the best of the crop of young players. They were the club that won the FA Youth Challenge Cup the first time it was competed for—in 1953, and they went on to win it every year until 1957 when other clubs began to get a look in. Wolves first, then Blackburn Rovers (with Mike England their centreforward) and then, two seasons in succession, Chelsea.

Chelsea in the early sixties were rich with young talent as Manchester United had been in the fifties. For both of them the supply seems to have dried up a bit in recent years, and both of them supply evidence of the way in which too many promising youngsters jostling for a few positions means that several have to seek the road to the top with other clubs.

It is interesting to consider for just a moment the number of star players today who served their time with Second or Third Division clubs and probably came into the first elevens sooner because of this—and were then transferred to top clubs. In the North West, to give a few examples, Liverpool's Alex Lindsay emerged with Bury and Kevin Keegan and Ray Clemence both with Scunthorpe, whilst my club-mate Colin Bell, like Lindsay, served his time with Bury.

Or there is the up and down career of Derek Possee—a youth player with Tottenham at a time when perhaps Spurs seemed a bit reluctant about throwing young players into the fray (they've changed over the past seasons with players like Steve Perryman, Jimmy Pearce and John Pratt getting early chances to prove themselves); transferred to Millwall and spending several seasons with them in the hope that they would reach the First Division; then, in his middle twenties, taking the plunge and being transferred to First Division Crystal Palace.

At the Palace, of course, Possee became a club-mate of Don Rogers, a player who had been content for many, many seasons to stay with Swindon, a club out of the top flight and out of the big population areas. With Swindon Don Rogers had enjoyed a few moments of great triumph as when Swindon beat Arsenal in the Football League Cup Final of 1969 but it is arguable that staying with them reduced his chances of playing for England—and that must be the ultimate recognition for a player.

My road was a somewhat tortuous one. As a youngster at Fulham I was with a First Division club—and playing in the company of Johnny Haynes. Then I was transferred to Queens Park Rangers—coincidentally with Allan Clarke coming to Fulham from Walsall. Fulham, in any case, soon dropped out of the First Division, whilst with Queens Park Rangers I shared in the ascent from the Third to the First Division—and, in 1967, in a Football League Cup Final, victory over West Bromwich Albion at Wembley (the first time the final of that competition was contested at Wembley).

Q.P.R., as I expect you remember, had only a short stay in the First Division and I suppose it did seem that, for me, events had meant that I was destined to play in the lower divisions of the

Iam McFaul, Newcastle's keeper, and Rodney Marsh in action

Football League—with a reputation as an 'entertainer' and a crowd-puller but no more than that.

Then Malcolm Allison stepped in and signed me for Manchester City—back in the First Division from 1966-67, league champions in 1967-68, F.A. Cup winners in 1969. A club, in other words, not only established in the top flight but one determined to show the world that football in Manchester did not begin and end with United at Old Trafford.

Soon after I arrived at Maine Road I admitted in an interview that I felt that 'It was going to be great playing in City's team and I want to do spectacular things for them.'

And that remains my attitude. More than that, Rodney Marsh, the entertainer and crowd puller, is now very much part of a team. Maybe that is why, or to some extent why, the England honours have followed with, as I write, appearances as a substitute against Switzerland and West Germany (at Wembley) and then, in my own right, against West Germany away, Wales, Ireland, Scotland and Wales again.

With luck, whatever the road I took—or was forced to take—I hope to be with England when they regain the World Cup in 1974 in West Germany.

Rodney Marsh, playing for England, eludes a tackle by Scotland's Billy McNeill

THE ALL STARS QUIZ
set by
Julian Jeffery

The chunky white shirted player is Coutinho but for what country did he play? (see Question 2)

Ten years have passed since I compiled my first **All Stars Quiz**, and while preparing the questions for this year's Annual I have been glancing through the teasers we have posed over the decade. By way of a change perhaps you would like to try some . . .

Imagine you are a football reporter . . .

1. To avoid making too frequent references to the name of a club in writing match reports, journalists often find it useful to call a club by its nickname. What club would you be referring to if you used the following nicknames?

    a) The Bees,
    b) The Gunners,
    c) The Magpies,
and d) The Shakers.

2. A football journalist needs to have a working knowledge of foreign as well as British football. Can you name the countries for whom the following famous internationals play(ed)? . . . Remember, this question was written ten years ago so although you should have no problem with the first player you may well need to reach for the record books in order to identify the others . . .

    a) Eusebio,
    b) Coutinho,
    c) Masopust,
and d) Gento.

Imagine you are a Manager . . .

3. Against which clubs would your team be playing in away matches at the following grounds?

    a) Maine Road,
    b) Craven Cottage,
and c) Hillsborough.

4. Imagine you are appointed team manager of the England side for a foreign tour of three matches. The first game is played at the famous Bernabeu (Chamartin) Stadium; the second at the San Siro Stadium; while in the final match of the tour your England team meets the national side of a country who came to prominence in 1962 when they reached the Final of the World Cup, only to go down 3-1 to Brazil. To what European countries would this tour take you and your team?

The All Stars quiz for 1966 asked you to find the players in two teams specially picked for an imaginary representative match between a Football League XI and a Rest of the World XI. Many of these players are still delighting football crowds, while others have since retired but their reputation has made them 'soccer immortals'.

Can you identify any of these players? Remember the clues were written eight years ago, but the answers may be easier than you think.

5. Goalkeeper for the Football League team ... this young Irish international, who turned in some great displays for Spurs last season, was bought from Watford for £27,000 in June 1964.

6. Number 10 for the Football League ... European Footballer of the Year in 1964, he has captained Scotland and Manchester United, who paid Turin £115,000 for him in July 1962. He was first capped in 1958, at the age of 18, and has also played for Huddersfield and Manchester City.

7. Rest of the World goalkeeper ... this star goalkeeper gave a great display at Wembley in 1963 playing for the Rest of the World against England. He has excelled many times when representing the Soviet Union and the leading Russian club, Moscow Dynamo. Typical of this big-hearted sportsman was his willingness to make the long journey from Moscow to Stoke to play in the Stanley Matthews Testimonial match.

8. Inside-left for the Rest of the World ... perhaps the greatest player in the World, the Brazil and Santos star with the passport that reads Edson Arantes do Nascimento ... but you know him better as ... ?

Of course 1966 saw England's success in the World Cup, and our quiz for the following year reflected the excitement this had aroused.

9. England's top goalscorer hit a hat-trick in the World Cup Final against West Germany. Who is he? For which club does he play (1966-67)? And what was the result of the Final played at Wembley Stadium on Saturday July 30th 1966?

10. Can you name the England team that beat West Germany in the 1966 World Cup Final?

In 1968 we posed a couple of questions about 'Crowd Records'. Do you know the answers?

11. The highest paying attendance at a football match played in the United Kingdom was recorded in 1937, when 149,547 people watched England go down 3 goals to 1 against Scotland. Where was this game played?

12. On October 12th 1935, 82,905 people attended the First Division match between Chelsea and Arsenal. However, the highest Football League attendance was recorded in January 1948 when a crowd of 82,950 watched Manchester United play Arsenal. At what ground was this game played?

1970 brought the World Cup under the spotlight again. This time the final stages of the competition were staged in Mexico, the location of the '68 Olympics. Naturally enough our quiz was devoted to the World's top football tournament.

13. When did England first enter the World Cup, and in which country was the Final staged?

14. England's first ever World Cup match (final stages) gave them a 2-0 victory over Chile. However, a few days later they received one of the greatest humiliations in world football history. On the little Belo Horizonte ground, despite continual English pressure, the United States of America beat an England team that contained many famous football personalities, including Billy Wright, Tom Finney, Jimmy Dickinson, and (Sir) Alf Ramsey. What was the score on this historic, if surprising, occasion?

After our trip back through ten years of All Stars Quizes, and I hope you found these questions interesting, even if they were a little hard, we'll finish with some straight forward questions, questions directly concerned with the past couple of seasons.

15. England were beaten 3-1 on aggregate in the quarter-finals of 1971-72 European Championship by the eventual winners of the competition. Which country won the Final, who were their opponents, and what was the score?

16. The European Champions Cup for clubs has been dominated in the 70's by two Dutch teams. In 1970 Feyenoord of Rotterdam beat Celtic

The now familiar exchange of pennants—this time before the start of the 1972 European Cup Winners Cup Final. Does this help you answer question 17?

2-1 in the Final, while in 1971 and 1972 the other leading Dutch club, from the capital city, Amsterdam, was victorious in both Finals beating Panathinaikos of Greece at Wembley, and Inter-Milan the following year. Can you name the club?

17. English teams have a fine record in the European Cup-Winners Cup, but Scotland's first success did not come until 1972, although the club concerned had twice been losers in the Final. Which club?

18. 1972 also saw the first all English European Final when Spurs and Wolves met in the UEFA Cup. What was the aggregate score in the Final?

19. Colchester United sprang a surprise at the start of the 71-72 season, winning the Watney Cup. The same competition also provided a shock opening to the 72-73 season, another club from the lower divisions of the Football League beating both Second and First Division teams. Can you name the club concerned?

20. Finally, a simple question to close our quiz. May 1972 saw Leeds United finish runners-up in the First Division for the third year in succession. Which club pipped them in the Championship race?

Answers on page 109

69

Not a continuation of the quiz but there is a puzzle about these two pix. Who is the keeper with the straddled legs disappearing beneath his Millwall opponents? And what (oppo) is Jimmy Hill doing running the line? Answers: Graham Horn of Portsmouth. Jimmy volunteered to run the line when the official linesman at an Arsenal-Liverpool match tore a muscle

70

Chris Lawler (No. 2) poised to catch the leaping Kevin Keegan after the latter has scored the winning goal for Liverpool at West Ham's Boleyn ground.

MILESTONES IN MY SOCCER LIFE

by Steve Heighway

Steve Heighway in action in the 1971 F.A. Cup Final against Arsenal

WE WERE CONFIDENT THAT WE COULD STILL PULL OFF A VICTORY—ANOTHER INSTANCE OF THE SHANKLY TOUCH RUBBING OFF ON TO US

You can't win them all—but Liverpool seem to make a habit of winning most of their games. That's been my experience, since I signed as a professional footballer for the Anfield club. Obviously, much of Liverpool's success is due to the manager, Bill Shankly, whose attitude towards the game rubs off on to the players. 'The boss' never acknowledges defeat until the final whistle has been blown, and it's an attitude of mind that he has instilled into the men who wear Liverpool's red jersey.

I've been surprised by quite a few things, naturally, in my comparatively short time in the game as a professional. One thing which makes me blink, when I stop to think about it, is the number of games I have played in just over two

This is where I work—a happy picture of Steve Heighway, B.A.(Econs), showing his wife, Sue, around Liverpool's famous Anfield ground

seasons—I was well past the century mark, before even half of last season had gone. That's another thing you come to accept at Liverpool—they are in so many competitions and they fight so hard to win them all that the games come and go in rapid succession. Last season, we were playing two matches a week for a large part of the season. If it wasn't a Saturday League match, it was a mid-week League Cup-tie or a European tie—and before the F.A. Cup came along, we'd played more than three dozen matches.

Naturally, when I look back over the past couple of years, I find that certain clubs and certain matches seem to mark milestones in my professional career. Tottenham Hotspur, for instance. Although I made my debut for Liverpool in a Football League Cup-tie, I made my bow in a First Division match at White Hart Lane.

It wasn't long before I was playing there again—this time in an F.A. Cup replay. Spurs had been drawn at Anfield in the sixth round, and it was a hard game. But although we felt we had outplayed them—and despite our claim for a penalty award, because we thought a Spurs defender had handled the ball in his own penalty area—Tottenham took us back to White Hart Lane for a replay.

I suppose most people imagined then that we had missed our chance of marching into the semi-finals. But the Liverpool players didn't think so; in fact, it was surprising how confident we were that we could still pull off a victory. I suppose that's another instance of the Shankly touch rubbing off onto us!

That Sixth Round replay was a milestone in my career because I scored the only goal of the game . . . and our victory took us on to another

Another happy moment for Steve Heighway—he has just scored the opening goal in the 1971 Cup Final and sub Peter Thompson runs to congratulate him. Alas, Arsenal grabbed an equaliser and won in extra time

milestone, so far as I was concerned. For our Semi Final opponents were Everton, who happen to be our No. 1 rivals. Everton mark more milestones for me, naturally. I remember my first taste of a derby game against them. It was at Anfield.

During the week before the game, plenty of people seemed to think there was nothing else to talk about. The match was THE subject, and yet, somehow, I couldn't feel as deeply involved as all that. I did get keyed up—as I always do—before the match, but even then, it was more or less another game, even if it was an important one.

Everton certainly showed no signs of an inferiority complex, and they delighted their supporters by going two goals up. It took a tremendous fight-back by Liverpool to tip the scales . . . but, eventually, we made it. John Toshack

scored, and I scored—and Chris Lawler popped up with a last-minute winner. And it was then that I really appreciated what victory in a derby game meant, to so many people!

The Liverpool supporters went wild, and as we reached the dressing-room, you could sense the elation all the Liverpool players were feeling. I was simply caught up in the whole atmosphere, and suddenly I realised exactly what it DID mean, to win a game against your greatest rivals. I thought of what would have happened, had we lost . . . half the citizens of Liverpool would have been in mourning for a week, and the dressing-room at Anfield would have been pretty well like a morgue.

This aspect of football was brought home to me again, after we had beaten Tottenham in that sixth-round F.A. Cup-tie, and we played Everton in the semi-finals at Old Trafford. There was no

Steve Heighway (white shirt) being chased by West Ham's Tommy Taylor

doubt about that game being another milestone in my footballing career, for it was my first season in top-class football, and there I was, just ninety minutes from Wembley. In addition, I had been honoured by being selected to play for the Republic of Ireland in an international match.

Old Trafford was a mass of people, half wearing the colours of Liverpool, and half those of Everton. Immediately we took the field, I felt gripped by the same feeling I'd had when I realised we had beaten Everton in that Anfield derby game. But this was another game, another occasion—and we hadn't won it, yet. We didn't

No—this is not Steve Heighway in action again. The white shirted player being challenged by Arsenal's Bob McNab is Leicester's John Farrington

look like winning it, either, as Everton once more streaked into a first-half lead, playing their football with flair and confidence.

But again that Liverpool grit showed through, as we got down to our second-half job of salvaging at least another chance to have a go at them. Everton had Brian Labone injured, which

was bad luck for them; but they were able to bring on a substitute, of course, and in any case, we felt that we were gradually beginning to take a grip on the game. Alun Evans was the man who struck the equaliser for us, and Brian Hall the player who whipped in the winner.

It was cheers for Liverpool, tears for Everton.

And what a feeling it was, to know that we WERE at Wembley. There, we came up against Arsenal, and for 90 minutes, the issue hung in the balance. When a goal came, I was the one to crack the ball home—and I honestly thought that that goal had won the F.A. Cup for Liverpool. But Arsenal had other ideas, and they equalised, then Charlie George came up with a winner.

So that was another milestone in my career—a milestone which was full of disappointment, yet it was also an occasion which I wouldn't have missed. We had come so close to preventing Arsenal from doing the double of winning the League championship, as well as the F.A. Cup.

Last season, there were a few more milestones to mark, in my football career. There was the Anfield victory against Everton, and there were three games in Cup-ties which will always stand out in my memory. Two of those games were against a team which has always given us a fight—Leeds United.

Leeds had knocked us off the F.A. Cup trail the previous season, and the season before that, they had ended our interest in the old Inter-Cities Fairs Cup. Last season, we had gone to Leeds and beaten them in the League . . . and then we were drawn against them in the League Cup, at Anfield.

We went ahead, and thought that so far as Cup fighting was concerned, we'd cracked it, third time lucky. But on the stroke of half-time, Leeds scored an equaliser.

In the second half, they went ahead, and it seemed that they had got the Indian sign on us again. But with only about 10 minutes to go, John Toshack salvaged a replay for us, and so we went to Elland Road. Once again, i suppose, few people gave us a good chance of winning, but as the referee was beginning to look at his watch, with full time looming, we won a left-wing corner. I curled the ball over into the goalmouth, and there was Kevin Keegan, unmarked, and soaring like a bird to nod the ball past goalkeeper David Harvey.

Which took us on to Tottenham . . . and TWO more games in quick succession against them. The first was at White Hart Lane, on the Saturday after we had beaten Leeds. It was a League match, of course, and everyone was wondering whether our League Cup replay would have taken it out of us. We had been topping the First Division table for a couple of months, with Leeds, Arsenal and Tottenham all pushing to nudge us off our perch.

That League game was another which will linger in my mind, for we played brilliantly—and once again, I scored a vital goal. It was the first of the game, and it came just inside the half-hour. Four minutes from half-time, Kevin Keegan popped another one past Pat Jennings, and although Spurs pulled one back, the damage had already been done. The game finished up Tottenham 1, Liverpool 2 . . . and everyone was waiting for our next encounter, nine days later—this time at Anfield, in the Football League Cup. Ninety minutes stood between Liverpool and a place in the semi-finals, the winners of the tie being drawn against Wolves, who had beaten Blackpool by the only goal in a replay. By now, you will appreciate why games against the Spurs seem to have had a special significance in my career.

Our League Cup tussle attracted more than 48,000 fans—and this time, it was Spurs who struck first, when Martin Peters slotted home a goal. But, as we had done against Leeds in the previous round at Anfield, we hammered away, and Emlyn Hughes struck a magnificent goal, to salvage another replay.

Quite frankly, it was a replay neither team wanted, especially as the game had to go on at White Hart Lane only 48 hours later. And believe me, the players were whacked after their efforts, for we had ploughed our way through heavy grounds twice, with a 4-3 victory over Birmingham on the Saturday, and the draw against Spurs on the Monday.

However, we buckled down to it again at White Hart Lane, but for once, even Liverpool couldn't keep up the pace, and to our disappointment, Spurs struck three times in the first half, and we were left with only a late consolation goal. We never stopped trying, but we just couldn't stage a repeat performance of our F.A. Cup victory, or our League win. So I just had to mark that League Cup replay down as one of the disappointing milestones in my career. Still, as I said right at the start, you can't win 'em all . . .

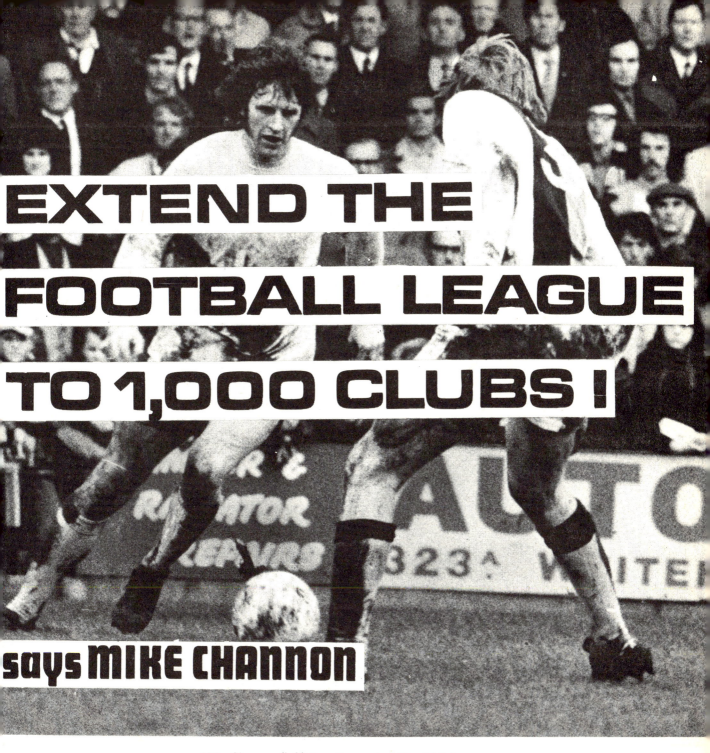

EXTEND THE FOOTBALL LEAGUE TO 1,000 CLUBS !

says MIKE CHANNON

Mike Channon (left) *in action against Crystal Palace*

I WOULD LIKE TO CONTRIBUTE SOMETHING TO THE GROWTH OF THE GAME—IF PLAYERS HAD THE CHANCE TO HAVE A SAY

Directors, administrators, managers and supporters have spent countless hours in the past year talking about how football can be revitalised. And I must say I've got a bit hot under the collar about it all at times—because nobody seems to worry about what the players think!

After all, it's the players who hold the future of the game in their hands. I think most profes-

Mike Channon and his wife, Jane, pictured soon after they moved into their new home at Southampton—handy for the Dell and for the hairdressing business that Jane supervises

Terry Paine, the Saints captain and long-serving player (more than 650 League appearances) in action against the Arsenal

sionals would have appreciated the courtesy of at least being asked for their opinions.

I've personally got a lot of ideas I would like to see tried out. And they don't just stop at Football League level. Sometimes I feel the people who run the League are too selfish—they don't seem to care what happens outside their own sphere. I think any reshaping of the game should be done on a much wider scale. Right down to the local clubs who, after all, are the grass roots of the game.

Some critics have said the Football League is too big; that some of the Fourth Division clubs should be thrown out. I take the other view. I think the Football League should be expanded

to include perhaps 1,000 clubs!

I think every senior club in the country should take part in what would really be a national league. The top three divisions of the Football League could be pruned to, say, 20 clubs in each section with three-up and three-down making life·more interesting. I certainly think we play too many games in the First Division.

After that we could have north and south sections of the Fourth Division, a Fifth Division in four regional divisions and a Sixth Division of perhaps eight groups. The whole thing could mushroom right the way down the scale so that the smallest club might be members of, maybe,

Peter Shilton of Leicester saves from Wolves' John Richards—highly rated by Mike Channon

Division Eight which would comprise 32 regional sections.

The success of new clubs Oxford United, Cambridge United and Hereford United soon after entering the Football League has been astonishing. And when I think of what some of the other hopeful non-League clubs like Wigan, Chelmsford, Barnet, Yeovil and the rest might have achieved *if they had been given the chance* I begin to wish that my ideas could be introduced.

Then every ambitious club would rise gradually up to its rightful position in football's social scale. The bad ones would sink, anyway. No need to consider voting out the less successful clubs. My plan would see them sorting things out themselves.

Don't think that I'm one of the panic-stricken people who believe the game is dying on its feet. Football has been going through a bad time, as far as attracting the spectators is concerned. But we have seen slumps before. These things go in cycles. I think some amount of re-organisation will come about—yet, the fact that the First

Division has only 20 clubs, instead of 22, isn't going to do an awful lot to increase gates is it?

In the end it is the players who must bring back the spectators. Playing fewer games will help us, of course. But I think we have to go on trying to improve our technique, trying to make the game more entertaining for the fans and, from my point of view in particular, I hope to bang in a lot more goals. Because goals, after all, are what the game's all about.

Goals are my business, of course. I'm paid to score them. But to do this I have to have the assistance of my team mates—and, in particular, my fellow strikers.

Very often the most successful strikers have come in pairs. We had Geoff Hurst and Roger Hunt working perfectly together in our 1966 World Cup winning team. Spurs were best when Martin Chivers and Alan Gilzean were on key together. I could quote many other examples.

At Southampton I worked up a very successful partnership with Ron Davies. And in the England Under-23 side I played with some of the best young strikers in the game.

Martin Chivers, once of Saints now of Spurs, in action for England against Greece at Wembley

It was my pleasure to play with John Richards, the Wolves' player whom I rate as the finest young prospect in the country. He truly is an outstanding player and I have only the highest admiration for him.

Joe Royle is another player I like to play with. He was alongside me at Wembley when I first played for the full England team against Yugoslavia. And, of course, we were partners in several Under-23 games. It's difficult to describe just what it was that made us click. We just seemed to get along well together and our styles suited each other.

Playing for England, particularly at Wembley, gave me great personal satisfaction though, strangely, I didn't really get any great thrill out of the occasion. I had been so close to selection before, and had nine Under-23 caps, that I felt sooner or later I would get that elusive first cap. In a way, I had come to expect the chance and had often thought about it, so the honour was not entirely unexpected.

One thing that playing for England did do for me personally was finally to get rid of my tag at

Southampton of being "a second Martin Chivers." I followed Martin into the Southampton side when he was transferred to Tottenham for a then record fee and many of our supporters used to call me that.

It used to annoy me a bit because I have never considered my style anything like Martin's. And, in my case, I did not like being considered a carbon copy of any other player—however famous.

Anyway, that's all behind me now. And, as Southampton's leading scorer for the past three years, I think I have proved a success in my own right.

Obviously, I hope to stay at the top for as long as possible. It would be nice to win more caps and perhaps pick up a Cup or League medal.

I would like to contribute something to the growth of the game, too. If players had the chance to have a say. There is talk about asking television and the pools to make even bigger financial contributions to football. There is even a suggestion that the government should be asked to subsidise the game. But, when we are talking about what everyone can do "for football", scant time is taken on asking what all these organisations can do for players.

What about players who have their careers cut short by injury? Or Fourth Division players, on small salaries, who come to the end of their playing days? Few of them have had training in any other job because the demands of modern football are such that you have to dedicate yourself to the game as soon as you leave school.

I think that the pools people could set aside some of the money they are prepared to pour into the game and put it into a Trust Fund which would look after players who go out of the game in difficult circumstances.

Newspapers and television go on about the huge amount of money earned by players. They don't make it too clear to the public that only a very small percentage of players are on the top whack. There are many players who have little money behind them when their playing days end. Then football conveniently forgets them.

This would be one of my priorities on any list of re-organisation. I hope the planners might agree with me. Better still—I wish they would allow us players to put forward officially our own ideas for improving the game!

A fine picture of Ian Hutchinson diving bravely to head despite the challenge of a Norwich player. Hutch after a long absence through injury scored twice for Chelsea but soon had to return to the injured list again

MORE FLAIR WANTED

STEVE PERRYMAN

Steve Perryman (right) *and Crystal Palace's Don Rogers in a chase for the ball*

. . . I FOUND THE NOISE ALMOST AN INSPIRATION THAT HELPED ME TO RAISE MY OWN GAME. BASICALLY YOU CANNOT BEAT THE ELECTRIC ATMOSPHERE OF A BIG MATCH

I suppose of all the present-day professional sports, football requires the most dedication and skill.

Nowadays, with all the European competitions we have to play in, tension both physical and mental, has become an integral part of the sport as a whole. So in other words if you are to succeed in football you simply must learn to relax.

Another London 'derby'—and two of London's brightest young players in opposition. Trevor Brooking of West Ham and Steve Perryman of Spurs

European football: The 'man in black', the Red Star Belgrade keeper, Petrovic looks back at his goal in which Martin Chivers has just slotted the ball for Spurs first goal in their 2-0 win in the Third Round of the 1973 UEFA Cup

Many of us of course have outside business interests, and many people say that our business activities regularly affect our performances on the park.

However, I believe that if you keep your business interests down to a minimum and try not to become too involved in their general activities, whether it be a shop or a restaurant, then it should help a player to cut himself off completely from the hurly-burly world of big time football.

I decided not too long ago to open a sports shop with my brother which I felt was an ideal proposition as my career is only just beginning, and this type of shop is just the right kind of outlet that can help me overcome any mental strains or tensions that I might have suffered after a big match. Yet at no time have I allowed my business in any way to destroy my football which of course my life is all about.

I have already mentioned European competition and the pressures which exist in such matches. But alternatively I do feel most strongly that playing in one of the European cups makes one a much more all-round player.

For example I will never forget the time we played A.C.Milan at the immense San Siro Stadium in the second leg of our UEFA Cup semi-final. There were approximately 85,000 Italians watching the tie, literally crying for our blood. And although I was fairly frightened during the first five minutes or so I soon found that as the game wore on I became more and more confident.

Also, in point of fact I found the noise almost an inspiration, and this helped me to raise my own game. So basically you cannot beat the electric atmosphere of a big match.

Essentially it helps you not only to raise your own game, but also to learn quickly to adapt yourself to strange surroundings, which is all part of the general education which every young player needs.

I know, and fully appreciate that there are people who are not at all keen on European competition. "Too many European cups," they say. But as far as I am concerned the more European football I play the better I will become equipped to represent England if Sir Alf decides to select me.

This of course leads us to professional football and money.

Not so long ago a leading national newspaper wrote in depth about the fantastic money made per year by the world's leading sportsmen.

Pelé £200,000; Jackie Stewart £150,000; Lester Piggott £50,000 plus. These figures certainly made my mouth water, and so did the fact that the 1970 Brazilian World Cup squad were reported)to have been paid £24,000 per man after their victory over Italy. Yes, all this big money certainly made me thoughtful.

What had happened to the incentives for British footballers? I asked myself. True, we are not badly paid, but our annual incomes and bonuses are still well below those paid to our counterparts in such basically poor countries as Brazil and Spain.

For instance a leading Brazilian oil company poured £500,000 into their World Cup squad. I fully appreciate that a great deal more interest was shown during the last World Cup by our own businessmen than is shown as other times, but it was still essentially small fry when compared with the lavish sums dished out to the Brazilians. I really cannot understand it because after all, before our squad went to Mexico we were still World Cup holders, and surely therefore our pool of players deserved all the support possible from business circles.

Of course several business houses are now taking a considerable interest in the future of British soccer—the Watney Cup, the Texaco Cup and the Bells Whisky Manager awards—are good examples of this. It took us an extremely long time to obtain sponsorship, so now let's use it and use it properly!

One of the troubles of this country is that even today there are many bitter people who resent the fact that we are no longer being paid £20 per week. What puzzles me is why such an affluent country as ours should in many ways

European football: but the opposition in the 1972 UEFA Cup Final is English. Alan Mullery pictured scoring Spurs winning goal against Wolves

Come and get it then—Spurs' keeper Pat Jennings seems to be inviting John Ritchie of Stoke

still lag behind the times footballwise.

We are rich, whereas countries such as Brazil, Argentina and Spain are poor. Professional footballers in the countries I have just mentioned have been earning large sums of money since before the Second World War.

But do their fans or officials resent it? Of course not. They are proud of their leading clubs and accept the huge financial rewards of their players as just part and parcel of the game.

Basically then English football is at the crossroads. Do we continue to play the hard-running, quick-breaking game based almost entirely on defence, or do we experiment more and play football as I feel it could be played, that is with the emphasis more on flair and improvisation.

To sum up therefore, I do feel most sincerely that the players should express themselves and not be over dictated by the many systems existing in modern firstclass soccer.

STARS OF EAST ANGLIA

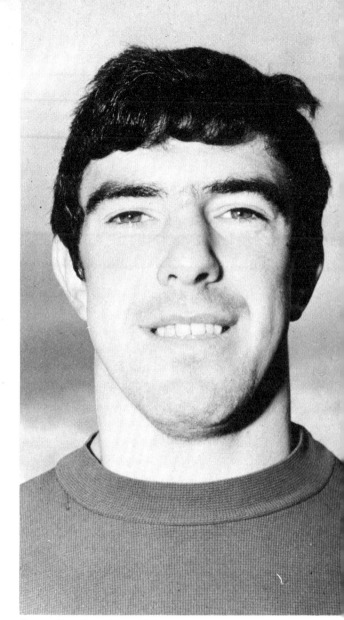

Mick Mills (Ipswich)

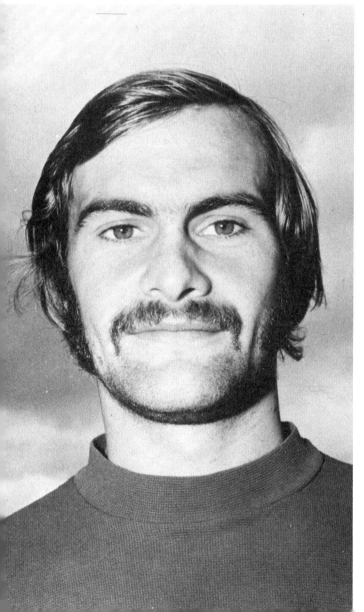

Bryan Hamilton (Ipswich)

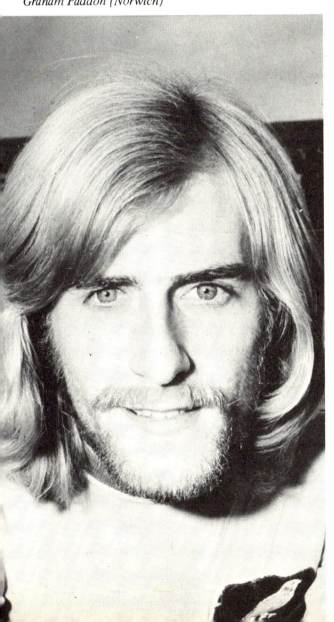

Graham Paddon (Norwich)

Duncan Forbes (Norwich)

WORLD CUP BIG THREE
Nobby Stiles

Heathrow—en route to the 1970 World Cup in Mexico. Emlyn Hughes (left), Jeff Astle, and Nobby Stiles *with a young autograph hunter*

I JUST WISH I WERE STARTING ALL OVER AGAIN AS AN ENGLAND INTERNATIONAL . . . BECAUSE I THINK WE ARE IN FOR SOME GREAT DAYS AGAIN

What chance have England of winning the World Cup in Munich, next year?—In my considered opinion, an excellent chance. I bracket them with West Germany and Brazil, as the three countries most likely to succeed. And having said that, let me add that I place Brazil third, because I believe that the boot will be on the other foot, for a change!

I'll explain . . . In 1966, when I was a member of England's World Cup-winning team, Brazil

1970 World Cup. Geoff Hurst in action against Brazil—Everaldo (left)

didn't make the finals. The tournament was held in England, of course, and it finished up as a battle between England and West Germany at Wembley.

I have two lasting impressions of that 1966 competition, apart from the winner's medal they will always be a concrete reminder of a day of glory for England and Nobby Stiles. My first impression, which still lingers, is how happy we England team-mates were together. Sir Alf Ramsey gave us something which money couldn't buy. At the time, people called it "togetherness" . . . and I wouldn't argue with that description. I've never been in a side like it, before or since. The whole build-up to the World Cup, and the atmosphere Sir Alf did so much to create among the players, made a real team of us—and I mean every single one of the players who was in

the squad.

My second lasting impression just goes to emphasise how wonderful the team spirit was. When we had beaten West Germany, in that dramatic Wembley final, the first bloke to rush up to me and offer his congratulations was Jimmy Greaves—yes, a fellow who didn't play. I knew just how disappointed Jimmy must have been, to have missed out on such a tremendous occasion, yet he was sporting enough to be glad for all of us, in our moment of triumph.

It wasn't all roses in 1966, as Jimmy well knows. Footballers, like other workmates, sometimes tend to disagree, and big Jack Charlton and I had a difference of opinion while we were training at Lilleshall. Can you imagine the two of us at loggerheads?—Jack stands more than head and shoulders above me . . .

1970 World Cup. Hottges (West Germany—No 2) and Bobby Charlton clash. Alan Ball in attendance

However, we didn't see eye to eye on that occasion, to the extent that we stopped playing football and started arguing the toss. Sir Alf stepped in to cool things down; he said quite firmly that it was right for us to have a go at each other, if we felt deeply enough about something, but that out on the park wasn't the place to do it. We should get on with the game, and then talk it out between ourselves, afterwards. And, of course, Sir Alf—as usual—was right. After that, big Jack and I forgot our differences, and became good friends—we both realised that what mattered most of all was helping England to win the World Cup.

The result of Sir Alf's endeavours became clear, as we worked and played together for England. Everyone felt a part of the squad, and anyone who was left out of the side didn't moan about it. Or if he did, it was to himself!

But I was talking about Brazil: and there is no doubt in my mind that, apart from having Pelé not fully fit for some games, and apart from their own failure to raise their game when it was vital, they found that conditions in this part of the world were not exactly 100 per cent to their liking. Which brings me to 1970 . . .

In Mexico, as I saw for myself, the conditions suited the South American teams much more than they suited the European sides. So Brazil were in their element from the start. And this weighed strongly against England, above all of the European countries, for in my estimation, we had the hardest group of the lot, to qualify for the final stages.

We had Rumania, Czechoslovakia and Brazil. And that little lot was a tough nut, in itself, even before we came up against West Germany. By the time England did meet the Germans, their efforts had taken a great deal out of them, and they were suffering from constantly having been drained of energy. You don't believe me? – Then I'll tell you something . . .

I got the surprise of my life, when Sir Alf named me in the England squad for Mexico. I'd been out of action through injury for a spell, and I'd only just recovered full match fitness. I'll never forget what Sir Alf said, though, when my name was included in the party for Mexico. "Nobby Stiles is good for England . . ." That gave me a real boost, I can tell you. I always loved being a part of the England set-up.

When England played Rumania – and they had one or two players who could do a bit of kicking – I sat in the stand. It was 4 p.m., and I was in the shade; and I was wearing a hat, because I'm not one of the sun worshippers. I managed to keep fairly cool – as I thought – about the game, but out of curiosity, I weighed myself when I got back to our hotel. I'd lost 8 lbs!

And when you consider that that was just through WATCHING the match, ask yourselves how the lads down on the pitch must have fared. They had no hats, they were right in the sun, and they were running around for 90 minutes.

When it came to the game against Brazil, I was in my track suit – as substitute. England put up a great performance, take it from me, even though they lost 1-0. Gordon Banks made the "miracle" save from Pelé, and Franny Lee sent a header just over the bar. But with 20 minutes to go – which was around the time that Brazil did get their goal – you could see that the England defenders were tiring; they could barely keep going, after the pace they had maintained for 70 minutes. Sir Alf realised this, too . . . but it was just as he was getting Colin Bell warmed up, to play in front of the defence and take some of the weight, that Brazil scored.

The Czechs gave us another hard game. England had to win this one, to qualify, and they managed it. But, even so, you could see once again that the lads were tiring, as the minutes ticked by. And by the time they came up against West Germany, the heat and the conditions generally had taken their toll. Even though we went into a two-goal lead against the Germans, Jack Charlton and I could see from

out seats in the stand that the defenders were starting to wilt again. And when West Germany made it 2-1, big Jack couldn't take any more . . . he walked out.

Well, it's history now how the Germans knocked us out of the 1970 World Cup. And they followed up by knocking us out of the European Nations Cup, with that victory at Wembley a year ago last spring. And I think that Sir Alf was "conned" for the first time in his life. Roy McFarland was out of action, and Sir Alf switched Bobby Moore to centre-half, instead of playing a recognised No.5.

That meant that, for once, England didn't play any ball-winners in the middle of the park, and Gunter Netzer was given freedom to use the ball. I believe Sir Alf played the team most people wanted him to play. I don't believe he did it because he thought people wanted him to play such a team; it so happened that his views and the majority view coincided, and so he didn't play a lone hand, as he usually does. But everybody is entitled to be wrong once in a while – and I may even be wrong in my opinion about the team which lost to West Germany.

So now we come to the jackpot question: what can England do in 1974? I've said I think they'll do well, and I've said it's between England, West Germany and Brazil, in my opinion. Brazil I bracket in third place, because I think that in Germany, as in England in 1966, they will find conditions don't suit them as much as they suit us. Which is what I meant when I talked about the boot being on the other foot. And they won't have Pelé.

I think England can beat West Germany, too, because we've learned our lessons against them, and because the men who play for us will be absolutely determined not to come off second-best again. Sir Alf is building up towards Munich just as he did for the 1966 and 1970 tournaments, and those who say he doesn't give players a chance are talking rot. He's experimented, all right, through the 10 years and more that he's been the guv'nor. Sir Alf aims to have a team just ready for the occasion; he doesn't want the players over their peak before the World Cup . . . he wants them in top form AT THE RIGHT TIME. And I think his team will look something like this, assuming Gordon Banks doesn't play in

After West Germany's unexpected quarter-final victory in extra time against England in the 1970 World Cup, the respective managers, Helmut Schoen and Sir Alf Ramsey, meet to commiserate and congratulate

goal: Shilton; Madeley, McFarland, Moore, Cooper; Todd, Bell, Ball; Royle, Keegan, Channon.

Colin Todd could win a reprieve, and he or Paul Madeley could play at the back or in midfield; or maybe Peter Storey and Emlyn Hughes will win places. Alan Ball's attitude is infectious, and I think he'll be there for his third World Cup.

As for the front three, I'm certain Kevin Keegan will play, and profit from Alan Ball's prompting; I believe Joe Royle will be a hot contender, if he's fully fit; and I think Mike Channon might just oust Franny Lee... although Franny seems sure to be in the squad.

I've gone for Peter Shilton in goal, because I think he's proved himself more than Ray Clemence. Ray may be the steadier 'keeper, but I think he's been behind a better defence at Liverpool than Peter has had at Leicester, and so Peter has seen more of the action, and this may go in his favour. Although I wouldn't grumble, whichever of these two fine goalkeepers got the vote. I'm sure they'll both travel to Munich.

Bobby Moore shows no signs of flagging, and he looks a cert to skipper England again, and right through the side I believe we shall have men of strength and craft, men who can win the ball and use it—and men who can strike for goal. Add to all this that determination I mentioned earlier and it sums up my reasons for believing that England will win the 1974 World Cup, and beat West Germany in the process.

I just wish I were starting all over again as an England international... because I think we're in for some great days again.

Liverpool's Kevin Keegan, tipped by Nobby Stiles for England's 1974 World Cup squad, being chased by big John Roberts, then with Arsenal, now of Birmingham City

BIG SPENDERS–Manchester United (see following article) were the biggest spenders last season but, usually with relegation worries, other clubs also splashed out on new players. Few made so many excursions into the transfer market as Crystal Palace whose 'purchases' included Charlie Cooke and Paddy Mulligan (above) from Chelsea, Alan Whittle from Everton, Derek Possee from Millwall, Don Rogers from Swindon, and from Dundee Ian Phillip–seen in action (oppo) against his fellow-Scot, Willie Carr of Coventry

(Above) *May 1971–Colin Stein of Glasgow Rangers in action against Celtic in the Scottish Cup Final.* (Right) *October 1972–Colin Stein again, a big buy for Coventry. In action for his new club against Crystal Palace. Ian Phillip is the Palace player behind Stein*

The Magic of Manchester United by STAN LIVERSEDGE

Manchester United fans 'take over' Wembley to see their team beat Benfica in the European Champions Cup Final 1968

... THE MAGIC OF MANCHESTER UNITED MEANS TOO MUCH TO TOO MANY PEOPLE FOR IT TO BE ALLOWED TO FLICKER AND FADE AWAY

This is the season when people will be looking more than ever for the results achieved by one particular team, on a Saturday evening. Manchester United. Tommy Docherty has had half a season in the managerial chair, and it didn't take long for him to make an impact. After only a few days as United's manager, he swooped to sign midfield man George Graham from Arsenal and full-back Alex Forsyth from Partick Thistle, in £100,000-plus deals that took Manchester United's spending to more than £800,000 on six players.

Ian Moore, Martin Buchan, Wyn Davies and Ted MacDougall were players signed by Frank O'Farrell, in his brief reign at Old Trafford, Tommy Docherty. enlarged the Scottish contingent when he snapped up Graham and, soon after, Forsyth; and in the first half of 1973, he got on with the job of trying to save Manchester United from relegation.

It was a remarkable tribute to the magic of Manchester United that, despite their many off-colour displays, despite their struggles and up-heavals, they continued to draw the fans wher-ever they played, even before Tommy Docherty took hold of the reins. For at the turn of the year, they had an average home League gate of more than 45,000, and their first league match with 'Doc' in charge brought 56,194 fans to Highbury—the highest attendance of the season at that stage.

United's name gained its magic under the managership of Matt Busby. He lifted the club to the pinnacle, during his years in charge at Old Trafford. They became a club famed for playing exciting, entertaining football; they produced a seemingly endless stream of stars—if they hadn't got them on their books, they went out and signed them, breaking transfer-fee records in the process.

Harry Gregg, Northern Ireland international goalkeeper with Doncaster Rovers, became the top-priced 'keeper in the game when he joined United, at a fee of £23,500. Albert Quixall, the golden boy of Sheffield Wednesday, became a £45,000 United acquisition. Paddy Crerand, of

Happy days for United. Sir Matt Busby and George Best embrace after the May 1968 victory over Benfica

Lou Macari after scoring for Celtic in the Scottish Cup Final, May 1972

Glasgow Celtic, was signed as a midfield creative artist, at £56,000; and another Scot, Denis Law, was bought back from Italy for £116,000.

United also had Bobby Charlton, Bill Foulkes, Tony Dunne, David Herd—and they took the wraps off an Irish footballing genius named George Best. They won League championships and F.A. Cup Finals . . . and, eventually, after 10 years or so of striving, they won the European Champions Cup.

I travelled with Manchester United on some of their European excursions—to Milan, just after the Munich disaster; to Belgrade, when everyone expected them to make it their year . . . and they came a cropper against the virtually unknown, unrated Partizan.

United rode the crest of a tremendous wave of public sympathy, after Munich, as they stormed through F.A. Cup ties to reach Wembley. In 1957, Stan Crowther played for Aston Villa against United at Wembley; in the 1958 final, he was lining up in the United side, as one of the new signings at Old Trafford.

United lost their European tie in Milan, and it was not surprising. After all, they WERE a hastily-assembled side, even though the team had been stiffened by the signing of little Ernie Taylor from Blackpool. Their energies were sapped by the heat, and the occasion proved too much for them, one way and another. But they were still Manchester United . . .

Matt Busby always managed to mask his feelings, always seemed able to produce a smile, no matter what disappointments his team suffered. But for once, the mask slipped—just for seconds—when United lost in Belgrade to Partizan. The game was there for the taking, in the first half, as Partizan seemed overawed by the mere fact that they were playing United; but United didn't seize the opportunity to go in for the kill. And after half-time, Partizan (maybe someone had made them realise United were only human, after all) came out and scored goals which were to prove winners.

That was the one occasion on which I saw Matt Busby's face without a smile, when I went to ask him for his comments, immediately after the game. He asked me to wait a couple of minutes, while he had a word or two with his players—and when he returned, the smile was back in place. He was ready to face the world again.

But in 1968, there was no need for him to mask any sorrows . . . Manchester United gave Benfica a 4-1 hiding at Wembley, and won the European Champions Cup. The whole football world rejoiced, because United had achieved their ambition, at last. And Busby and his players laughed and danced with joy.

Everyone knew it would be difficult to follow United's manager, when he stepped down. And so it proved. Wilf McGuinness had a go, and so did Frank O'Farrell. The magic of United's name remained, but the results didn't match their reputation last season.

And, as Christmas loomed, O'Farrell gave way to Docherty. A Scot who had managed half a dozen clubs, and the national side north of the Border. A Scot who was a former international, a class player with Preston and Arsenal, and who became the manager of Chelsea, to the surprise of many people in the game.

Tommy Docherty, hard but fair as a player, turned out to be a manager whose name was seldom out of the headlines. His ebullient nature, his ambition to achieve swift success for Chelsea . . . these were reflected in his wheeling and dealing in the transfer market, as he signed and sold players.

Tony Hateley was one of his signings. Hateley scored a goal which put Chelsea into the Final in 1967. The delighted Docherty couldn't hide his feelings, as he said: 'That's what we paid £100,000 for . . .' referring to the fee Hateley had cost, and what his goal had meant to Chelsea.

Football sometimes provides strange twists to a player's career. Alex Stepney, who finally succeeded Harry Gregg as Manchester United's goalkeeper, was signed by Chelsea from Millwall at a record fee of £55,000. The man who signed him was Tommy Docherty—and it was Docherty was, 112 days later, transferred him for a similar fee to Manchester United. At the time that Stepney arrived at Stamford Bridge, Peter Bonetti was there, and 'The Doc' proclaimed that he now had the two best 'keepers in the country. When he sold Stepney, Docherty admitted that he would have let him go to no other club than Manchester United.

Lou Macari after scoring for Manchester United in his debut match, January 1973

Stepney played but one First Division game in his 112 days at Chelsea. It was at Southampton, and Chelsea won. Alex told me about it, after his arrival at Old Trafford. He described how the team stopped for a meal on the return journey, and how Tommy Docherty bought each of the players who smoked a box of 50 cigarettes. It was a personal gesture which showed that Tommy Docherty can be a very warm human being.

George Graham, recently signed from Arsenal, expressing the determination that Tommy Docherty wants to recapture the glory for Manchester United

He could also be tough—he sent several Chelsea players home from Blackpool, for a breach of club discipline. And he was never afraid to plunge into the transfer market and back his judgment. Sometimes he surprised people by the way he splashed cash on players others didn't really rate; but his buys usually turned out to be sound investments.

Eyebrows were raised in some quarters, when Manchester United moved so swiftly to persuade him to become their third manager in as many years. Not that he needed much persuading. And while Tommy Docherty may make mistakes in the future—as he would be the first to admit that he has made some in the past—the new master of Old Trafford has demonstrated often that he is his own man.

Docherty has brought to Manchester United a different type of approach. Matt Busby always played it cool, and there were no fireworks. Tommy Docherty, as Alex Stepney discovered during his short stay at Chelsea, is a fast talker, and a good one. But, as the saying goes, he 'has all his chairs at home.' He knows the size and scope of the job he took on a few months back. He knows that nothing but the best will satisfy United, that they must make their way back to the pinnacle, in the shortest possible time. And that will be a task suited to the man in charge. He wasn't a slacker as a player, and he won't be a sluggard, as a manager.

What it boils down to is this: that the magic of Manchester United means too much to too many people, for it to be allowed to flicker and fade away. And in Tommy Docherty, United gambled that they had found a man not merely to restore the glitter, but to burnish it until it outshone every other club once more.

We all know what happened at Old Trafford, in the last few months of last season. But today, there's a sense of anticipation even greater than before, for Tommy Docherty was charged with the task of pointing the way upwards, when he arrived at Old Trafford . . . and that's why people will be watching for United's results more eagerly than ever, this season. After several years of in-between, United wanted to go places in a hurry; and in Tommy Docherty, they signed not just a manager, but a man of action geared to the challenge United thrust before him.

Ian Moore in action

PLAYERS ARE HUMAN BEINGS

BOB LATCHFORD

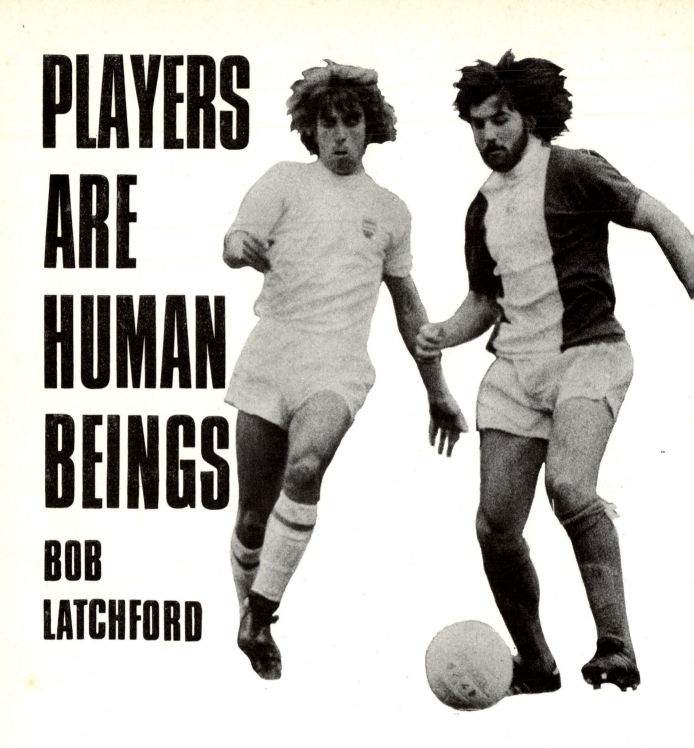

Bob Latchford (right) *in action for Birmingham against the Italian club, Sampdoria*

AS FAR AS MY INTERNATIONAL CAREER IS CONCERNED, THIS HAS GOT TO BE LEFT TO THE ASTUTE SELECTION OF SIR ALF RAMSEY

I feel that the complete combination of my own game, which I had been waiting like a guard dog for many years, came about at the end of the 1971-72 season.

For the first time during my years in professional football I actually trembled with emotion when I scored the winning goal at Orient, which enabled us to be promoted to the First Division. I suppose I was haunted throughout my career, and although my earnings had increased, there was nothing concrete to show for it.

As many of you know, Trevor Francis gained a corner and there was I to head the winner.

In a kind of way my career has always been shrouded by all sorts of aggravations. Yet that season, like a pedigree greyhound, we came in with a burst just as Liverpool had done in the First Division.

You see, many football scribes never at any time gave us credit for our all-round skills, both up front and in defence, although our success in gaining promotion was undoubtedly the result of a 100% effort from all the lads.

Like many young potential football stars, I realised early in my career that outside football, one is simply a human being with the same temptations as anyone else. And as such I have always tried to avoid making my personal life into a mess. Throughout the years, this mental state of mind has without question influenced my game tremendously.

Our manager at Birmingham, Freddie Goodwin, has an almost uncanny knack of being able to dispel any fears one might feel before a vital match, and his interest in all the Birmingham players, has in my view been one of the main reasons why we were able to overtake more fancied clubs to gain promotion to the First Division.

As far as my international career is concerned, this has got to be left to the astute selection of Sir Alf Ramsey. Will I achieve the ambition of any professional, you may ask? Well, my answer to this question is that if I continue to score goals regularly, who knows!

Answers to ALL STARS QUIZ on page 67

1. a) Brentford, b) Arsenal, c) Newcastle United, d) Bury.
2. a) Portugal, b) Brazil, c) Czechoslovakia, d) Spain.
3. a) Manchester City, b) Fulham, c) Sheffield Wednesday.
4. Spain . . . the Bernabeu Stadium is in Madrid; Italy . . . the San Siro Stadium is in Milan; and Czechoslovakia.
5. Pat Jennings . . . still turning in superb performances for Spurs and Northern Ireland. One of the top goalkeepers in the world.
6. Denis Law . . . a 'star' for so many years . . . a truly great professional.
7. Lev Yashin . . . perhaps the finest goalkeeper the world has seen.
8. The incomparable Pelé.
9. Geoff Hurst of West Ham (now Stoke) scored the hat-trick in England's 4-2 win over West Germany.
10. The England team was Gordon Banks, George Cohen, Jackie Charlton, Bobby Moore, Ray Wilson, Nobby Stiles, Bobby Charlton, Alan Ball, Geoff Hurst, Roger Hunt, Martin Peters.
11. Hampden Park, Glasgow.
12. Maine Road, the home of Manchester City (see question 3). Manchester United, who play normally at Old Trafford, had to use City's ground for several seasons after the war as their ground had been badly damaged in air-raids.
13. England first entered the World Cup in 1950 when the Final was staged in Brazil.
14. U.S.A. 1 England 0
15. West Germany 3 Soviet Union 0
16. Ajax
17. Glasgow Rangers
18. Spurs 3 Wolves 2
19. Bristol Rovers
20. Derby County

UP FOR THE CUP a flying header by Frank Worthington beats Bob Wilson in Leicester's Cup tie against Arsenal at Highbury